THERE'S MORE THAN ONE COLOR IN THE PEW

Dear Art,

It has been such
A blessing knowing you.
You are such an encouragement
to me. May the Lord continue
to bless you, brother.

In Him,
Tor
2009

TONY MATHEWS

There's More Than
One
Color
in the Pew

SMYTH&HELWYS
PUBLISHING, INCORPORATED   MACON, GEORGIA

Smyth & Helwys Publishing, Inc.
6316 Peake Road
Macon, Georgia 31210-3960
1-800-747-3016
©2003 by Smyth & Helwys Publishing
All rights reserved.
Printed in the United States of America.

Library of Congress Cataloging-in-Publication Data

Mathews, Tony, 1962-
There's more than one color in the pew :
a handbook for multicultural, multiracial churches /
by Tony Mathews.
p. cm.
Includes bibliographical references
ISBN 1-57312-415-X
(alk. paper)
1. Church work with minorities—United States.
2. Multiculturalism—Religious aspects—Christianity.
I. Title.
BV4468 .M38 2003
259' .089—dc22

2003014568

Contents

Acknowledgments 3

Introduction 5

1 Overcoming "Cold Feet" 7
  Before the Marriage

2 Common Denominators for 21
  Building Relationships

3 Mortal Combat and God's Diplomat..............31

4 Surface Integration Is Not Enough 45

5 Recruiting and Coaching..............................53
  the Dream Team

6 Confronting the "They Don't Do It Like Us"
  Syndrome 65

7 How to Scratch Itches Through 75
  the Worship Service

Bibliography 85

Leading a Seminar on Multicultural, ...91
Multiracial Ministry

Appendixes 99

Acknowledgments

Words cannot express my love and appreciation for my wonderful wife and children. For fifteen years, Angela has been a solid rock for me. Angela, thank you for your prayers and encouragement during the tough times and the great times. Michael, Nicole (Ryann), and Moriah, you are the best children any father would ever want. Thank you so much for your prayers and support during the writing of this book. It is dedicated to you.

The members of North Garland Baptist Fellowship have been wonderful to me throughout the past eleven years. Thank you for giving me the freedom to do what I love. You are a great church and I feel extremely blessed by God for having been called to serve you.

I especially want to thank the focus group members who spent several weeks assisting me with theoretical and practical research. We had a great time together! A significant portion of this book would not have been possible without your input and time. Thank you from the bottom of my heart.

Also, I am grateful to W. J. Subash for the time you dedicated in assisting me with editing this work. May the Lord bless you!

Introduction

Pastors, lay leaders, conventions, associations, seminaries, and Bible colleges, *get ready*! People from different cultures and races are not only moving to the same neighborhoods, they are also attending the same local churches. The need for pastors to care for multicultural, multiracial congregations is growing. Additionally, the laypeople in such congregations need skills to care for one another.

There's More Than One Color in the Pew analyzes the pastorate from a multicultural, multiracial perspective, addressing barriers that impede growth and relationships among the laity. Furthermore, the book outlines biblical and anthropological principles for multicultural, multiracial ministry. It presents the challenges and successes of pastoring different cultures and races. Both the practitioner who pastors integrated congregations and the congregations experiencing racial and cultural transition will find this book invaluable. Building on *Pastoral Counseling Across Cultures* by David Augsburger, which stresses that pastors should be intercultural people, *There's More Than One Color in the Pew* teaches pastors and the laity how to be intercultural.

Research reveals a need for books designed for pastoral and lay care in multicultural, multiracial contexts. George Barna, founder and president of Barna Research Group, has conducted demographic and marketing research for many secular and religious organizations worldwide. He has written a book titled *The Second Coming of the Church*. In one chapter, "The New Cultural Realities," he says that the church must understand and embrace cultural diversity. The Census Bureau informs us that while three out of four Americans are presently Caucasian, by 2050 only half of the nation will be Caucasian. For this reason, Barna adds, multiculturalism will be increasingly significant in our language, customs, values, relationships, and processes.

He further states that the church cannot afford to ignore the realities of cultural diversity. The outreach methods and procedures that were effective in the past are no longer relevant to a racially and ethically diverse population. The values and needs of each group are radically different; worship, evangelism, Christian education, stewardship, and discipleship goals must be tailored to the needs of each group. *There's More Than One Color in the Pew* addresses these areas and more. Consequently, I believe that the primary audience (church leaders) should invest in this book.

Manuel Ortiz, author of *One New People* and Professor of Ministry and Missions at Westminster Theological Seminary, also recognizes the growing need for churches to minister with some degree of cultural competence. He believes that "as the world continues to find its home here in the United States, we are being challenged by the sovereign God to practice the love and justice of our Lord in a multiethnic society." Training current and future leaders to provide pastoral and lay care in integrated contexts confronts many professors. Therefore, the second audience to which this book has value is theological institutions. Such institutions could use it as a supplementary resource book.

This book is structured for use by individuals or small groups in a local church setting or seminary setting. At the end of this book, however, you will find a guide for implementing a larger church seminar that develops skills for pastors and leaders toward a multicultural, multiracial ministry. State conventions and local associations throughout America are planting churches cross-culturally. *There's More Than One Color in the Pew* can be used to equip those who train pastors, churches, and lay leaders to implement, nurture, and grow multicultural, multiracial churches. The helps provided for this seminar will hopefully lead you and your growing and changing church toward developing cross-cultural, cross-racial relationships.

CHAPTER ONE

Overcoming "Cold Feet" Before the Marriage

The prophet Samuel was correct—"to obey is better than sacrifice" (1 Sam 15:22). Can you imagine how many people are content by their outward deeds without obeying the inward call to minister in a specific way? We often make this mistake in our walk with God in reference to the command to obey. Though tithing, visiting the sick, delivering messages, and other religious acts fetch us an "A" on our spiritual report cards, they do not guarantee the absence of "cold feet" when it comes to accepting people from races and cultures other than our own. As Christians, we must not, however, allow outward deeds to eclipse our inward call to minister to various races and cultures.

"Cold feet" is a sociological phenomenon that has left a deep scar in our society. Its influence is manifested in the churches, dividing worship communities on racial and cultural grounds. As part of the Great Commission, Christians have been called to bridge the differences and heal this "cold feet" factor.

I. Accepting the Call
The Importance of Ministering to All Races

My children were riding scooters outside with other kids in the neighborhood. All of them were laughing and talking as they wore themselves out from their hard play. As you know, kids seldom play together without quarreling. On this particular day, I heard arguing and crying. I walked outside and asked what was wrong with them. "She called me a name," said one of the kids. "I didn't call you a name," said the other kid. A third kid replied, "You did call him a name." The kid who was crying said to another, "You like them better than me." I asked the kids to sit down and then talked with them about treating people with respect and dignity. I told them that one kid is not better than another and we must all love each other. The manner in which I attempted to settle their quarrel was significant because these kids were from different races and cultures. They also live in the same neighborhood, and they happened to be at my house with my own children. I had been giving care to this diverse group of kids on this particular day.

Ethnic groups are not only moving to the same neighborhoods, but they are also on some occasions attending the same church—the house of God. As pastors and leaders, we have a responsibility to care for God's children who come to God's house. As in the case of the children in my neighborhood, God's children may play together, cry together, fight together, and often misunderstand one another as part of their growth. For this reason, pastors and leaders must be equipped for ministering to diverse congregations. Such equipping is vital because the individuals receiving pastoral care have expectations. They expect spiritual leaders to minister with some degree of cultural competence.[1] Likewise, God expects spiritual leaders to love and nurture their congregations.

Pastors and church leaders have special qualities. Among these qualities are the ability to sense the heart of God and to sense the desires God has for the church. In God's heart is a plan for multicultural, multiracial ministry.[2] For example, God told Abraham, the patriarch, "Go forth from your country, and from your relatives and from your father's house, to the land which I will show you . . . and in you all the families of the earth shall be blessed" (Gen 12:1-3). This word *families* refers to more than the simple family unit consisting of father, mother, and children. It signifies extended families or ethnic groups. It is also translated "all peoples" (NIV).[3] God's plan, which involves blessing God's people, is not limited to the descendants of Abraham. To the contrary, Abraham's descendants were to be God's vessels of blessing to all other people groups on earth. Again, God told Abraham, "And in you all the families of the earth shall be blessed" (Gen 12:3). God repeats this multicultural, multiracial plan at least once to Abraham (Gen 22:18), to Abraham's son Isaac (26:4), and to his grandson Jacob (28:13-14). Moreover, prior to the destruction of Sodom and Gomorrah, God repeats the plan to himself (Gen 18:17-18). Such repetitions not only reveal the redemptive plan of God for all nations, but they also reveal the passion of God for multicultural, multiracial ministry.

Pastors and leaders, I hope that you grasp this plan of God for God's people. It is happening all around us; the heart of God is literally unfolding in our churches. What are you going to do when different races and cultures come to the church you pastor? What happens when your neighbor, whose race is different from yours, wants to become a member of your church? Are you equipped adequately to execute the plan of God? Or are you saying, "I don't know how to minister to people who are not like me"? Regardless, you strongly sense that God is calling you to multicultural, multiracial ministry. Don't worry about the above-mentioned inadequacies, for many pastors feel this way. This is why it is important to understand certain fears and anxieties associated with the call to multicultural, multiracial ministry.

Fears Associated with Obeying the Call

I have heard horror stories about people getting "cold feet" right before their marriage ceremony. What an awful feeling for a bride or a groom! No doubt, mother throws the pots and dad kicks the car when the fiancé says, "I can't go through with it." I wonder what goes through the mind of someone who *bails out* of becoming part of something so special. One of the important factors in a person getting cold feet before marriage is fear. Providing pastoral leadership to a congregation is like holding together a marriage relationship.

It also resembles the relationship between shepherd and sheep. In the context of a church, anxiety and fear arise when the sheep are different colors.[4] Nearly twenty years ago, in San Angelo, Texas, I was encouraged to provide pastoral care to an integrated group. During this time, I worked second shift at a Johnson & Johnson company. Due to the nature of my job, each week I rotated seats that resulted in my being placed next to someone of a different race. By the grace of God, I shared my faith and led many people to Christ. Among these people were African Americans, white Americans, Filipinos, Mexican Americans, Puerto Ricans, and people from Vietnam and Korea.

As a result of my ministry among these people, I was asked to conduct a midnight service, once a week, for nearly one hundred people. I said to myself initially, "No way! There are too many different cultures and races. It's okay to lead them to Christ, but I cannot provide pastoral care to them." I tried to convince myself that I was not the person for the job, and deep in my heart, I was scared to death. The thought that I would be providing leadership to a multicultural, multiracial group was frightening. I am sure there are many pastors who have similar feelings when faced with pastoring different races and cultures. From my experience, I've culled a list of common fears and suggestions for combating them.

Do I preach well enough for the other race?

When presented with the idea of a mixed congregation, pastors have said, "It is hard enough to preach to one race, but now I have to preach to several races!" Don't worry. More than likely, the people have heard worse sermons and better sermons than ours. Accept and build relationships with these people. They value the relationship more than your messages.

Will they accept me?

Pastors top the list of those who want to be accepted. Though this is a true and legitimate fear, I encourage you to be yourself. One way to discourage the congregation is trying to be someone you are not. I often think about the leadership of Moses before he obeyed God's call. He was afraid to accept the call of God to go to Egypt (Exod 3). Observe the courage he gained: "a mixed multitude also went up with them, along with flocks and herds, a very large number of livestock." This mixed multitude was a multicultural, multiracial group that benefited from Moses' vision and leadership (Exod 12:38).

I don't understand their culture.

Although not having knowledge about someone's culture is a legitimate fear, it provides us with an opportunity to learn about another culture. During my San Angelo days, I had a good Vietnamese friend named Tran. He was aware that I knew nothing about his culture. To do my part to nurture our relationship, I had to overcome my ignorance. When I sat next to him at work, I asked many questions about his customs and traditions; he enjoyed and appreciated my curiosity. I also asked him to teach me how to say, in Vietnamese, simple words like hello and good-bye. In fact, I did this with friends of all cultures. My willingness to learn simple words fostered our relationship and enhanced my ability to provide them with pastoral care. I continue this practice today at North Garland Baptist Fellowship, a multicultural, multiracial congregation.

Can I keep the church integrated?

Once people from different cultures begin attending your church, you may feel the need to keep the racial mix balanced. This pressure is indeed fearful because you feel as though you are failing God and the multicultural, multiracial cause if the racial mix does not remain balanced. Listen, my friend: it is not your job to keep the church integrated. Though we are intentional at building a multicultural, multiracial ministry, ultimately *God* adds members and keeps the church integrated.

Two Obstacles to Successful Integration

I am reminded of two experiences that were both bitter and sweet—bitter because so many people still have not accepted other races, and sweet because so many people have already accepted other races. I present these two examples because I believe that as the black/white relationships improve, race relations all over will improve. My intent is not to speak in a condescending way toward one race or culture, but be aware that the primary speed bump in the road leading to multicultural, multiracial ministry is people. Humans can discourage others from obeying the call to minister cross-culturally and cross-racially.

"I didn't know the pastor was black!"

In 1994, members of the church I pastored were excited about having our first worship service in our new building. Electricians, carpenters, and construction workers were completing their work. While I was in my office, the church's door opened. My secretary, a white female, greeted a man who was excited. He stated that he and his wife watched the construction of the church and that they were eager to attend service this coming Sunday. He praised the beauty of the steeple, brick, windows, carpet, and sanctuary. Then he asked about the pastor. My secretary gave the man her opinion as to what type of pastor I am. She also mentioned to the gentlemen that I was attending seminary in Fort Worth, Texas. My secretary asked him, "Do you want to meet the pastor?" He exclaimed, "Yes! I would love to meet the pastor." At this time, I walked out of my office and approached the man. I extended my hand toward his, but the handshake never occurred. Instead, the man examined me from head to toe, viewing me with disbelief. He stated that the church looked nice and that he would like to come and visit. Next, he asked, "Who's preaching this coming Sunday?" I replied, "I am." He then said, "It was nice meeting you." I had a strong feeling I would not see him in our first service, and I did not.

After this encounter, I went back to my office saying to myself, "This multicultural, multiracial ministry is not going to work." Ten minutes later another white couple entered the church. They spoke with a member about the beauty of the steeple, brick, carpet, and sanctuary. Afterward, the member asked them, "Do you want to meet the pastor?" They exclaimed, "Yes!" The couple was directed to my office, and I said to myself, "Here we go again." But to my surprise, the white man extended his hand to me first, and we shook hands. This couple spent a significant amount of time talking with me, and they attended the church for years.

"I don't want to worship with whites!"

A few weeks after our church opened, I called visitors to thank them for attending the church. I called an African American gentlemen and asked if he was interested in joining. He said, "Nothing can make me join that church." He further stated that he worked with whites all week, and he did not want to see white folks on Sunday morning. He said the music was not black enough, the worship was not black enough, and the church was not black enough. It was obvious to me that this guy was not going to visit us again. I kept making calls that resulted in me speaking to another African American man. Before I could ask how he liked the service, he exclaimed, "I've been looking for a multicultural church." He proceeded to say so many good things about the church to the extent that I was trying to get off the phone; this was a sweet experience.

I took a few lessons from these encounters. Avoid judging an entire race or culture based on your negative experience with a member of that race or culture. Also, always thank God for the different races and cultures attending your church. Concentrating too much on people who do not unite with the church can limit your pastoral care to loyal and faithful members.

Your Proven Call to This Ministry

"How," you may ask, "do I know I am called to multicultural, multiracial ministry?" This is a good question. You must look for inward and outward evidence. When the Lord was calling me to this ministry, I remember a nagging feeling inside my gut. It felt as though a foreign object was invading my private, content, and satisfied Christian life. When something foreign enters your life, the natural response is to reject it. I had attempted to reject this specific call, but God kept calling me back. The pestering and nagging call from God validates the inward call that cannot be resisted. Here are questions for you: Do you have a nagging, pestering, and annoying feeling in your gut when you avoid multicultural, multiracial ministry? Or are these feelings present in your life, but you have not pursued the idea of such a ministry? Only you know the answers to these questions.

Outward evidence is another way of knowing if you are called to multicultural, multiracial ministry. If you pastor a church situated in a neighborhood with diverse races and cultures, the answer is "yes," you are called to this ministry. If your church is in a mono-cultural neighborhood and people from various backgrounds consistently travel to your church, such action is outward evidence that you are called to multicultural, multiracial ministry. Let me hasten to say, however, that some churches will not be able to integrate totally. Several years ago, I was contacted by a congregation in the state of Washington. They wanted to know if I was interested in becoming their pastor. Members on the search committee told me that the church members were all white, the people in the neighborhood were all white, and the surrounding communities were all white. They said I would be the only member in the church who was not white. Geographical factors determined the racial and cultural profile of this church. On the other hand, there are monocultural churches that exist in multicultural neighborhoods. In such cases, pastors and their churches will have to answer to God in respect to the intentionality of their mission toward inclusiveness.

Jesus Obeyed the Call to Minister Cross-culturally

"And he had to pass through Samaria" (John 4:4). The phrase *had to* points to the divine appointment. The road through Samaria was not solely a short-cut leading to Jesus' destination. He intentionally went through this area with the purpose of breaking down barriers that existed between Jews and Samaritans. Such a mission was on God's agenda, and Jesus obeyed the call to minister cross-culturally. Would it not be great to know God's will for your life and to obey it? Would it not be great to obey God as Jesus did? Would it not be great to break down barriers as Jesus did? I know what some of you may think: "Jesus was God, and we cannot obey God as he did." I have good news for you. You can obey God as Jesus did. Since we are believers, the Holy Spirit lives in us, enabling us to obey God's will. You can do it! Where is your Samaria? Find it, go through it, and break down those racial barriers!

II. Specifics of the Call
A Call to Assist Interracial Children

I begin this section with a letter that highlights the need for pastors and leaders of churches to provide care to people of interracial families. Such families are confronted with many challenges. Therefore, leaders need training in order to care for these families as they confront various mind-sets in society.

I received the letter from one of our members. She sought information concerning interracial relationships. During this member's first semester at a Christian college, many people told her that interracial relationships are not biblical. As a result, she started inquiring into the topic. It was obvious that she was both hurt and confused. Her parents are interracially married and she is the offspring of their relationship.[5]

> Pastor Mathews,
>
> How are you? I hope everything is well. Things are going well and swiftly at this school. It is a nice school, although it has its ups and downs. My classes aren't too hard, yet! I still have not found a church home here. There is no place like North Garland Baptist Fellowship! I feel so weird in a church that is a majority of one race! I thank God North Garland is so diverse. Pastor Mathews, I have a question for you. Is there anywhere in the Bible where God speaks about not mixing tribes? A lot of people here say that God speaks against interracial relationships. I have not been able to find my answer. I hope you can help me so that I could express to these people that God does not have a problem with interracial relationships (I think).

My response to her:

Dear Member,

Hello, and how are you doing? I received your letter on last Friday and here is my response. You asked, "Is there anywhere in the Bible where God speaks of not mixing tribes?" The answer is yes. "Now therefore, make confession to the LORD God of your fathers, and do his will; and separate yourselves from the peoples of the land and from the foreign wives" (Ezra 10:11). Exodus 34:14-16 says, "For you shall not worship any other god, for the LORD, whose name is Jealous, is a jealous God lest you make a covenant with the inhabitants of the land and they play the harlot with their gods . . . and you take some of his daughters for our sons, and his daughters play the harlot with their gods . . . ." So, the answer to your question is yes, God does speak of not mixing tribes. However, you need to know why God spoke against mixing tribes.

God spoke against mixed marriages (above Scriptures and more) for spiritual reasons, not cultural or racial reasons. The basis for the condemnation of mixed marriages was not racial or ethnic, but spiritual. The foreigners worshiped false gods, and our God did not want His people marrying and mingling with them. Remember, God does not want these marriages because of spiritual reasons not racial reasons.

Now, let us turn our attention to your next comment, "A lot of people here say that God speaks against interracial relationships." Listen carefully. God speaks "against," but not against interracial marriages. God speaks against those who speak against interracial marriages, especially if God put the marriage together. For example, Moses had a wife from a different race, a "Cushite wife." Moses' brother and sister spoke against this interracial marriage (Num 12:1ff). In verse 9, "the anger of the LORD burned against them . . . ." Miriam was punished with leprosy and Aaron confessed his sin and admitted that he and Miriam behaved "foolishly" (Num 12:11). It is a big mistake to conclude that God promotes racial separatism. People who speak against interracial marriages need to be very careful. They may be speaking against what God has ordained. Stay strong and keep up the good work.

These days, this young lady is doing excellent in school and has adjusted well to her new environment. Now let us turn our attention to bringing other races into the church.

Implementing a Multicultural, Multiracial Project in the Church

Since pastors all over the world need to care for multicultural, multiracial congregations, and since these congregations need the necessary skills to care for one another, I conducted a project that involved pastoral and lay care in an integrated context. The focus of the project was the local church where various cultures relate and interact.

The practical application of the project involved a group of members from different cultural and ethnic backgrounds. This group analyzed the pastorate from a multicultural, multiracial perspective as well as barriers that impede growth and relationships among the laity. Furthermore, the group assisted me in outlining biblical and anthropological principles for multicultural, multiracial ministry. It reported the findings and recommendations to the church body for enhancing Christian multiculturalism, pastoral care, and understanding the effects of ethnocentrism. We will hear from this group in various chapters throughout this book.

You and your church can adapt this section and other sections to your own context and conduct a similar project. Prior to implementing the project, you should meet with church leaders and explain to them the importance of conducting such a project in your church. I met with the deacons and presented testimonies and illustrations concerning multicultural, multiracial ministry. We discussed newspaper articles that highlighted the need for churches to receive people regardless of race or culture. Three weeks later, we introduced the project to the church. At this time, less detailed stories of multicultural, multiracial ministry were presented. I gave an overview of the project and entertained a motion from church members to affirm and conduct it.

After the vote, the members received a project schedule that included a brief explanation of the sessions. Having the schedule and the proposed sessions in their hands excited the members. We explained that everyone would be a part of the project, but there would be a limit to the number of people who could be included in the focus group. Afterward, a few members asked if they could indicate, by electronic mail or fax, where they wanted to serve. This request was made because they wanted to serve in the focus group and they did not want to wait until the following Sunday to choose.

Although the ownership covenant (see Appendix A) is a way to overcome this obstacle, I recognized that the covenant needed changes. Instead of

OVERCOMING "COLD FEET" BEFORE THE MARRIAGE

members choosing one area in which to serve, it was determined that they should indicate their first and second choices on the form. The change was made and the ownership covenant and feedback forms were reduced to fit inside the church bulletins. The following week, the members of the church chose the areas in which they wanted to serve. Afterward, the focus group members were selected and letters were sent to everyone who made a selection.

Church Members Who Answered the Call to Dialogue Cross-culturally

A focus group consisting of eighteen people spent twelve weeks interacting and conversing on cross-cultural, cross-racial issues. The group includes five white males, six African American males, three African American females, and four white females. One of the white men is from Swedish lineage and one is from German lineage. Also, one of the African American males' home country is Nigeria. Additionally, one white woman is married to an African American man and they have a biracial child. A white male is married to an African American woman and they have a biracial child. The Nigerian male is married to an African American woman and they have three children. One of the white focus group members has two white biological children and two adopted biracial children. The group consists of people who are part of the paid and volunteer staff, and others are part of the laity. Deacons and leaders of various ministries are also represented.

Members A-D

A is a white male between 36 and 45 who works with the music department. *B* is a white male between 22 and 35. He is a member of the laity. *C* is a white female between 46 and 55; she works in the Christian education department. *D* is an African American male between 36 and 45. He is an assistant minister at the church.

Members E-I

E is an African American female between 36 and 45. She is part of the laity. *F*, an African American female between 36 and 45, is part of the laity. *G*, a white male over age 55, is part of the laity. *H* is a white female between 22 and 35; she is part of the laity. *I* is a white female between 46 and 55. She is part of the laity.

Members J-N

J is an African American male over age 55; he is part of the laity. *K* is a white male between 36 and 45. He serves as a deacon at the church. *L* is from Nigeria and between 46 and 55. He is a deacon at the church. *M* is an African American male between 36 and 45. He is music minister of the church. *N* is an African American male between 22 and 35. He is the youth minister of the church.

Members O-R

O is a white male over age 55 who serves as a deacon. *P* is an African American female between 36 and 45 who serves in the Christian education department. *Q* is an African American male between 36 and 45 who serves in the discipleship department at the church. *R* is a white female over age 55 who teaches Sunday school.

It was a joy to see these focus group members grow in their understanding of the concepts of multicultural, multiracial ministry. Among other things, they studied pieces of Scripture which are relevant to the subject of multicultural, multiracial churches, they identified differences between homogeneous and multiethnic congregations, and they developed strategies for diminishing barriers which divide Christians across racial and cultural lines. Throughout this book, you will learn about these individuals. This was a great group of people who helped me more than they know.

NOTES

[1] Vergel L. Lattimore, "The Positive Contribution of Black Cultural Values to Pastoral Counseling," *Journal of Pastoral Care* 36 (1982): 106.

[2] In my preliminary studies, I used only the term "multicultural." However, some congregations are both multicultural and multiracial. Therefore, the terms "multicultural, multiracial" are used throughout this book.

[3] To assist me with formulating a biblical foundation in various parts of this book, I used H. Connor Goerner, *All Nations in God's Purpose* (Nashville: Broadman Press, 1979).

[4] "In scriptural imagery, 'sheep' represent prized persons, created in God's image, who are beleaguered and burdened. These were persons from all races and classes of humankind who were 'harassed' and 'oppressed.' They filled the city streets, thronged the marketplaces, and walked the rough pathways of Palestine. Pastors today feel similar pulls of the people upon their own personalities, thus need to share ministry to achieve the church's mission" (C. W. Brister, *Pastoral Care in the Church* [New York: HarperCollins Publishers, 1992], 35). For further discussion of the sheep/shepherd motif, see pp. 35-36.

[5] For a critique of interracial marriages, see the pamphlet *Marriage Across Barriers of Religion, Race and Culture* (Nashville: Christian Life Commission), 5-6. This pamphlet gives several reasons why people should not marry outside their race. Such reasons are social and not necessarily biblical. The pamphlet, however, can be used for informing couples during premarital counseling sessions as to the various attitudes that exist in our society regarding interracial marriages.

DISCUSSION QUESTIONS

1. In Genesis 12:1-3, to what does the word "families" refer?

2. How many times does God mention the multicultural, multiracial plan in the book of Genesis? List the Scripture references.

3. What fears do you have when you think about implementing or staying in multicultural, multiracial ministry?

4. In your own words, explain the outward and inward evidence of being called to multicultural, multiracial ministry. Give personal examples of each.

5. Why did Jesus not hesitate to go to Samaria? What lessons do we learn from him?

6. Why do you think people disagree about interracial marriages? Are you aware of interracial marriages in the Bible with which God was pleased?

CHAPTER TWO

Common Denominators for Building Relationships

Do the names Herman Boone and Bill Yoast mean anything to you? One was African American and the other was white. In the early seventies, they coached a group of kids to the state football championship in Virginia. Initially, tension existed among the players because their skin colors differed. However, the team successfully worked through their racial problems because they had one thing in common—football.

Now do you remember Boone and Yoast? That's right. They were characters in the film *Remember the Titans*, which was based on a true story. I recall watching this film and saying to myself, "If football can bring together different races and a town that is saturated with prejudice and biases, surely the body of Christ should come together because of our common denominator—Jesus Christ." Meeting people on common ground is possible because it was Christ who "made both groups into one, and broke down the barrier of the dividing wall" (Eph 2:14).

I. Common Ground

Why Meet People on Common Ground?

Shortly after the turn of the twenty-first century, *Christianity Today* cited a New York Times poll that revealed racial divisions in worship: 90 percent of whites reported that there were few or no blacks in their worship services, and 73 percent of blacks reported that their congregations had few or no whites. About the same time I read this article, I was given a book titled *The Millennium Bug*. It was written to prepare people for the coming chaos of the twenty-first century—the Y2K problem. In the introduction, the author wrote, "Don't worry . . . you can bet that someone a lot smarter than either one of us will come up with a solution for this. If we can put a man on the moon, we can certainly fix the Y2K problem."[1] He was right! The Y2K problem was fixed. But here is an important question. If we can put men and women on the moon, should we not be able to fix another millennium bug—the Sunday morning segregation problem? If pastors, church leaders, seminary professors, Bible colleges, and the laity will invest their time and effort into solving this problem, we can make much progress. Moreover, someone a lot smarter than us, Almighty God, developed the solution a long time ago, and he encouraged people from diverse backgrounds to meet one another on common ground. Such encouragement is recorded in various biblical texts.

Exodus, the second book of the Pentateuch, reveals how the Hebrew people became a nation. Additionally, this book reveals the "constitution" or the Ten Commandments that would govern their lives (Exod 20). God's reason for giving the "constitution," or Ten Commandments (19:3-6), supports the nature of this book—namely, multicultural, multiracial ministry. Prior to giving the Ten Commandments, God spoke these words to Moses:

> And Moses went up to God, and the LORD called to him from the mountain, saying, "Thus you shall say to the house of Jacob and tell the sons of Israel: 'You yourselves have seen what I did to the Egyptians, and how I bore you on eagles' wings, and brought you to myself. Now then, if you will indeed obey my voice and keep my covenant, then you shall be my own possession among all the peoples, for all the earth is mine; and you shall be to me a kingdom of priests and a holy nation.' These are the words that you shall speak to the sons of Israel." (Exod 19:3-6)

How does this statement involve multicultural, multiracial ministry? First, God says, *for all the earth is mine* (19:5). The context suggests that God is talking about people on the earth. These people represent various cultures, races, nations, and tribes. Second, the context reveals that God has a plan for such people. More importantly, the accomplishment of this plan involves the function that the nation of Israel is to perform. God told Moses that they would be *a kingdom of priests* (19:6); therefore, they would function as *priests.*

The function of a priest is no small matter. The priest is a mediator between God and the people. Additionally, the priest reveals the will of God to the people and makes the people acceptable to God. Exodus 19:3 reveals that God wants a kingdom of priests—a nation composed entirely of priests—that ministers to the other nations (Gentiles) and peoples of the world. This is part of God's plan for humanity. Moreover, notice the response of the people after hearing God's plan for them. They said, "All that the LORD has spoken we will do!" (Exod 19:8).

Centuries later, Peter communicated the same plan to a multicultural, multiracial group. This group consisted of Jews and Gentiles scattered throughout Pontus, Galatia, Cappadocia, Asia, and Bithynia. He wrote, "But you are a chosen race, a royal priesthood, a holy nation, a people for God's own possession, that you may proclaim the excellencies of him who has called you out of darkness into his marvelous light; for you were once not a people, but now you are the people of God; you had not received mercy, but now you have received mercy" (1 Pet 2:9-10). Both Jewish Christians and Gentile Christians are now God's people, and both receive his mercy.

Fostering Common Ground Discussions

"How," you may wonder, "do I begin to meet someone on common ground? I have no idea where to start because we have nothing in common." This is an honest assumption. However, you probably have more things in common with people who are racially and culturally different from you than you realize. A more technical exploration of our commonalties is recorded under the heading "Similarities and Differences" below. For now, let us look at practical common denominators for building cross-cultural relationships.

On-the-job training

One of the best places to identify what you have in common with other races is your place of employment. People love to talk with others between breaks and during lunch hours. The intentional conversationalist, during these discussions, will discover similarities he or she has with other races and cultures. The key word is *intentional.* For example, when you speak with someone, always ask yourself these simple questions: Do I agree with this person? Do I know someone who agrees with this person? Have I experienced what I am hearing? Is this person reaching out for help? With what areas of this conversation do I agree? Ask each question with the primary objective of determining what you have in common with the other person.

Hobbies

I'm a big sports fan, and my son is rapidly becoming one too. Several months ago he played basketball in a local league. Once a week, the boys practiced while the parents watched. During a particular practice, I heard one of the parents (a white male) talking about Buffalo, New York—my hometown. When the opportunity presented itself, I told him I had heard him speaking to another parent about Buffalo and I wanted to know if he had roots there. He proceeded to tell me that he went to college there, and the other parent (an Asian American man) was raised there. A black man, a white man, and an Asian American man, all of whom are in Texas with sons on the same basketball team, have a connection with Buffalo, New York. This was not a coincidence. One of the parents and I talked every week during the practices and games. Several months after the season was over, he called me and requested me to minister to a friend of his. This is one way God works in our lives when we intentionally look for common denominators with other races and cultures.

Jesus Met a Member of a Different Race on Common Ground

"So he came to a city of Samaria, called Sychar, near the parcel of ground . . . and Jacob's well was there. Jesus therefore, being wearied from his journey, was sitting thus by the well" (John 4:5-6). Wells were used as meeting places in the ancient world. They were places where people encountered one another. Therefore, it is no small matter that "there came a woman of Samaria to draw water" at Jacob's well (John 4:7). This was a divine appointment for the woman. Jesus knew that Jews and Samaritans did not like one another, but beneath Jesus' weariness and thirst was his desire to break down racial walls. He accomplished this by meeting the Samaritan woman on common ground. What did they have in common in this context? He was a man but she was a woman! He was a Jew but she was a Samaritan! They both, however, had at least one thing in common: the Jews loved Jacob and the Samaritans loved Jacob. This is why Jesus met her at Jacob's well. Where is your Jacob's well? Who will you meet there? It may be the football field, a shopping mall, or a garage sale. The key point here is to meet people on common ground.

II. Similarities and Differences

Do Different Races Understand Racial Terms the Same Way?

In chapter 1, I mentioned that I spent twelve weeks with a cross-cultural, cross-racial group in order to discuss various issues related to race. I also provided a profile on each person. This segment takes you inside our meeting and reveals our conversations and interactions. One question presented to our focus group was, "Can people struggling with 'prejudice' work with other people in a multicultural, multiracial church?" Although not unanimous, the group responded that if people have a desire to change, they can work in such a context.

The key word for the focus group members was "struggling." Focus group member *F*, an African American woman, believes that "a prejudiced person can get to know and understand other cultures by working with them." Focus group member *J*, an African American male, believes that "the struggle he or she is having may not be a threat against the church . . . we should allow them a chance. We may be able to minister to them and help them remove their prejudice."

The members immersed themselves in dialogue about the word "prejudice." This resulted in me supplying the group with a definition of the word (see "Getting Started" in the seminar notes). After the group discussion, each group member presented a response to the question. Member *M*, an African American female, and member *Q*, a white male, were in the same group. *Q* said, "We agreed on everything except the question pertaining to being prejudiced." Addressing the focus group, *Q* said he told *M* that he was prejudiced and that this disclosure disturbed *M*. *Q*, elaborating on his disclosure, said he admitted he was prejudiced prior to reading the definition supplied to the group. After examining the definition given, *Q* said, "I'm not prejudiced in that way." It was obvious to me and the entire focus group that these two individuals, who are from different cultures and races, had different meanings in mind when discussing this term.

This is significant because the African American related the term to what Webster describes as "an irrational attitude of hostility directed against an individual, a group, a race, or their supposed characteristics." The white male related the term to what Webster describes as "preconceived judgment or opinion."[2] This was a significant event for the focus group because it revealed not only that people are different, but also that they use important terms in distinct ways. We realized the need to clarify terms in order to foster healthy cross-cultural and cross-racial communication. Furthermore, we were provoked to consider whether African Americans are more defensive when conversing with white Americans due to injustices of the past.[3]

Similarities in All People

Jerry Appleby succinctly identifies several ways in which human beings are similar.[4] First, there is a *biological similarity*. Appleby argues that the stereotyped differences of race, color, features, and stature are inconsequential because "human anatomy (including blood types), reproduction, and all bodily functions are primarily the same worldwide." Second, there exists an *intellectual similarity*. "Perception, memory, reasoning, emotion, and volition are almost identical among all humans."[5] Moreover, one must consider the *spiritual similarity* in humans. Appleby believes humans are spiritual beings. He believes the universal need of all humans is to receive salvation and be transformed.

I added a fourth similarity, namely, *eschatological similarity*. By this I mean that each individual, regardless of ethnicity or culture, will one day die and face the Maker of us all. The writer of the book of Hebrews states, "it is appointed for men to die once and after this comes judgment" (Heb 9:27). One day we all will stand before God and give an account of the things we have done on earth (2 Cor 5:10). Understanding that these similarities exist among humans in general, and Christians in particular, is vital when ministering in a multicultural, multiracial setting.

Theological Reflections

Several theological principles are relevant to this book. They involve the origin of humanity, the image of God in humanity, the universal nature of sin, and the extent of God's love. Such principles play a key role in understanding multicultural, multiracial ministry. The subject of humanity is the starting point for reflection.

The origin of humanity

The word of God teaches that all humanity descended from a single pair. The narrative of the creation of Adam and Eve, along with the genealogies in Genesis, reveal this teaching (Gen 1:28; 3:20, 5). Also, Genesis 1:1–2:3 tells of the creation of all things and presents humans as the climax of creation (1:26-30). That humans are the climax of God's creation reveals certain truths. First, humans differ from the rest of the creation in the sense that several particulars, mentioned below, are not seen in the creation of other living things. Second, humans as the climax of God's creation helps our understanding of Christ (since the Bible teaches that the Second Person of the Trinity became a human). To understand Christ's human nature, one must understand the nature of humanity.[6] Examining these particulars reminds integrated and homogeneous churches that humans should be treated with great dignity and respect.

The image of God in humanity

Many biblical passages address the image of God. One of the most familiar passages is found in Genesis: "And God created man in his own image, in the image of God he created him; male and female he created them" (1:27). The New Testament instructs believers to "put on the new self, which in the likeness of God has been created in righteousness and holiness of the truth" (Eph 4:24). Paul tells the Colossians that they "have put on the new self who is being renewed to a true knowledge according to the image of the one who created him" (Col 3:10). To be created in the image of God is a theological issue that has received various treatments from theologians and scholars. However, what is known about the image of God, in terms of humans being created in God's image, enables one to declare that human beings are unique individuals.

Human life is sacred; because of this sacredness, all humans deserve respect. The Bible says, "Whoever sheds man's blood, by man his blood shall be shed, for in the image of God he made man" (Gen 9:6). Scripture condemns murder because such an act destroys one made in God's image. Therefore, murder constitutes a sin—not merely against the victim, but also against God.

Also, since humans are made in the image of God, one should put forth one's best effort to be in harmony with God and with other human beings. I describe such harmony as "vertical" and "horizontal wellness." Horizontal wellness, or harmony among humans, reaches its fullest potential when people submit to God and to each other in the fear of Christ (Eph 5:21).

Erickson maintains, in commenting on the image of God, that "we experience full humanity only when we are properly related to God."[8] Those who serve in multicultural, multiracial churches desire to win people to Christ so that people can have this proper relationship. Furthermore, multicultural, multiracial churches believe that when people are properly related to God, reconciliation and healthy relationships between different cultures occur.

The common ancestry of humans

Humans are not only made in the image of God, but they also have a common ancestry. The Bible states, "and he made from one, every nation of mankind to live on all the face of the earth" (Acts 17:26). John B. Polhill, commenting on this text, writes, "Although there are many nations, though they are scattered over the face of the earth, they are one in their common ancestry."[9]

J. W. MacGorman calls such commonality the "affirmation of the unity of mankind." He states, "Paul cut across the grain of Greek pride and prejudice by stating that God had made from one man (Adam) every nation on the face of the earth."[10] In that same vein, F. F. Bruce affirms that "all mankind was one in origin—all created by God and all descended from a common ancestry."[11] David Augsburger indicates that "we are all much more alike than unlike."[12]

Such theological reflections reveal the interconnection of humans. Such a connection motivates those who serve in integrated churches to love and share Christ with humanity. Although our oneness, by virtue of creation, is admirable, there is a deep desire to see humans eternally connected, by virtue of the second birth. Therefore, let's continue to spread God's word until Christ comes!

NOTES

[1] Michael S. Hyatt, *The Millennium Bug* (New York: HarperCollins Publishers, 1992), xi.

[2] *Webster's Ninth New Collegiate Dictionary* (Washington, DC: Regnery Publishing, Inc., 1998), 928.

[3] Reconciliation is also a goal for those who counsel cross-culturally. At times, however, obtaining reconciliation is difficult due to barriers erected by one race that has been hurt by another race. Benoni Silva-Netto writes an article that examines whether or not American pastoral counselors, when counseling, should promote keeping a uniform cultural system or embrace and understand the cultural diversity present within society. Silva-Netto uses the term "Hermeneutic of Suspicion" to describe the attitude some ethnic groups have that derives from negative experiences with other races. For further information, see Benoni Silva-Netto, "Pastoral Counseling in a Multicultural Context," *Journal of Pastoral Care* 2 (1992): 136.

[4] Jerry Appleby, *The Church Is in a Stew* (Kansas City: Beacon Hill Press, 1990), 38-39.

[5] Of course, if Appleby means that we all have exactly the same memory and the like, that could be refuted.

[6] Millard Erickson, *Christian Theology* (Grand Rapids: Baker Books, 1985), 456.

[7] Leon Wood, *Genesis, Bible Study Commentary* (Grand Rapids: Zondervan, 1975), 26.

[8] Erickson, *Christian Theology*, 515. See the extended discussion on the implications of the image of God. Also, Erickson summarizes the universality of the image of God (515-17).

[9] John B. Polhill, *Acts, The New American Commentary* (Nashville: Broadman Press, 1992), 374. Polhill believes that one can see the significance of this in an address before Gentiles. The God whom Paul proclaimed was no local Jewish cult God. He was the one sovereign Lord of all humankind. Polhill also believes that God made every human nation, and that every human comes from Adam.

[10] J. W. MacGorman, *Acts, The Gospel for All People* (Nashville: Convention Press, 1990), 82-83.

[11] F. F. Bruce, *The Book of Acts* (Grand Rapids: Eerdmans Publishing Company, 1988), 337.

[12] David Augsburger, *Pastoral Counseling Across Cultures* (Philadelphia: Westminster, 1986), 49. Also, Yale University has compiled material from 300 cultural groups that reveals 88 categories of universals in human nature (51).

DISCUSSION QUESTIONS

1. According to Exodus 19:6, what does God tell the people they will be to him?

2. What New Testament writer talks about a royal priesthood? In your own words, explain how these Old and New Testament passages correspond to God's multicultural, multiracial plan for humanity.

3. What are some things you can do to meet members of a different race or culture on common ground?

4. What did Jesus and the Samaritan woman have in common? Why is this important?

5. Do you think a person who struggles with prejudice should be a part of a multicultural, multiracial church?

6. Name three ways the author believes human beings are similar and three ways you believe human beings are similar.

CHAPTER THREE

Mortal Combat and God's Diplomat

The argument has been over for hours and there is still silence in the house. "We need to talk," said Marsha. James said, "OK, what do you want?" Gently, her hand took his and she led him to his favorite spot—the rocking chair. Marsha sat down on the carpet and said, "James, you know that you were wrong, but I love you. You are a great man and I pray that after you think about the way you handled this situation, you will see that you could have handled it in a different manner." Marsha's smile, her caring words, and the "favorite spot" disarmed James's bad attitude and resulted in him asking for forgiveness. Paul's words are correct. "The Lord's bond-servant must not be quarrelsome, but be kind to all, able to teach, patient when wronged" (2 Tim 2:24).

I. "Care-fronting" Conflict

Most people have directly experienced some sort of conflict in the church. If you are a pastor who says, "I never faced any problems within the church,"

keep pastoring and your time will come. The question is not "Will I experience conflict?" but "How do I handle conflict when it comes?" This question is important when providing care for different races and cultures.

Vital Information about Conflict

Wilmot and Hocker, in *Interpersonal Conflict*, write about "metaphors that expand conflict potential." These metaphors put a positive spin on conflict. Whenever I experience conflict, I use one of their metaphors and remind myself that conflict is like a *garden*.

> In creative conflict, as in good gardening, seeds are planted for future growth, pests are managed, weeds are pulled, and the garden is watered when needed. Sun and light are needed for the plants to grow, and the most fruitful outcomes occur when the conditions are carefully tended. If constructive conflict can be seen as a garden, many positive outcomes can be experienced. In good gardening, poisons are not put on the ground—thus, rage, fury, and attacks, which are poison in an ongoing relationship, become as unthinkable as putting dry-cleaning fluid on rose bushes. In good gardens individual plants are given room to grow . . . people learn to leave space for others, to give them room to grow.[1]

In multicultural, multiracial ministry, people need room to grow. Some people from varied backgrounds have never worshiped or served together in the local church. This can present challenges. Some people have difficulties building relationships with others, not because of race, but because of personality. This can present challenges also. A keen leader recognizes these growth needs and establishes measures to deal with potential conflict among members. Moreover, a good leader works hard to determine, within a congregation, if the root cause of a conflict is people-related or race-related.

People-related or Race-related?

The first step in determining the root cause of conflict is to avoid certain traps. First, there is the *emotion trap*. Sometimes we respond to a conflict solely as a result of our feelings and make false assumptions based on our impulses. Such responses can destroy a local congregation and cross-cultural relationships.

We must also avoid the *commotion trap*. Unfortunately, members gravitate toward people who are at conflict with others. Many people who gravitate are not interested in helping solve the problems but serve as agitators and perpetuators of the conflict. Ignore all forms of communication that attempt to play the race card without solid evidence that indicates the conflict is race-related.

Another trap to avoid is the *cessation trap*. People who cease to serve in a church because they experience conflict with members of a different race are in this category. As a result of conflict, too many individuals cease to use their spiritual gifts and talents for the kingdom. Sadly, they may be hurting themselves.

A final trap to avoid is the *termination trap*. Victims of this trap say, "I'll move my membership in order to avoid dealing with this conflict that involves another race." This is one of the worst actions a person can take. Certainly, God leads each of us to the church he wants us to attend. Still, I do not believe God wants us to leave a church because of minor conflicts. In addition, the chance that there is conflict between people at the other church is high. So hang in there and be a part of the solution until God leads you in a different direction.

Having said this, how can we determine if the root cause of conflict is race-related? The information below is based on my experience providing pastoral care to integrated churches. These are observations and should not be used to judge the hearts of individuals. Ultimately, only God knows the heart.

Historical profile

Consider compiling a history of your members. Remember, multicultural, multiracial churches must be unapologetically intentional. Many times such churches must be unconventional in the way they provide pastoral care. Knowing portions of a person's past and recent history may lend support when determining if conflict is race-related. For example, many years ago a couple joined the church I currently pastor. After the couple left the church, it was brought to my attention that one of the spouses was reluctant to join because he or she was not accustomed to dealing with a certain race of people. In fact, I was told that this person did not like the particular group of people due to negative experiences from his or her past. It was also brought to my attention that shortly after the couple joined, the one spouse had several conflicts with members of the particular people group. If our leadership had been informed about this person's struggle with a particular race, we could have provided specific care and perhaps prevented the couple's departure. Keeping a profile is important. This process should be the first part of the new members' assimilation process or new members' classes. In these classes, avoid asking blatant questions about racial issues (i.e., "Have you ever used the 'n-word'?" or "Have you ever been a victim of racial profiling?"). Questions like these may prohibit instead of promote a smooth assimilation of members into the multicultural, multiracial church. Instead, include questions like the following on a new member questionnaire:

1. Have you ever been a member of a multicultural, multiracial church?
2. What attracted you to this diverse congregation?
3. How much experience do you have working with people of a different race or culture?
4. What negative experiences have you had with members of a different race or culture?
5. Do you wish to speak with a member of the pastoral staff about such experiences?

These questions are harmless, and the answers will provide the leadership with race-sensitive information about the people who join the church. Also include questions that are not race-related. Finally, remember that simply because a person had a negative experience with a member of a different race does not mean that person is the cause of conflict. The historical profile is part of the whole when determining the root of conflict.

Theological profile

Do you know what your members think theologically about multicultural, multiracial churches? What are their biblical views regarding different cultures and races worshiping together? You can discover these views during Bible studies, group discussions, and personal discussions with members of the congregation. All leaders in diverse congregations should know where their members stand on this issue. If individuals have a problem biblically or theologically with multicultural, multiracial churches, do not be surprised if their thinking influences their behavior with other people. Although rare, at times I have traced the root cause of conflict back to theological and biblical presuppositions regarding race.

Personal profile

Keep an account of your personal contact with the people. Church leaders should know their members. Spend time with them and their families. Observe how they interact with members of different races. I know that this sounds like a lot to do, but I cannot stress enough the importance of knowing your people.

Each of these profiles can be used to determine if the root cause of conflict is people-related or race-related. Now, what do you do if a problem is race-related? How do you deal with a person who is in a conflict because of his or her outlook on color?

Nine Ways to "Care-front" Racial Problems

When addressing those in conflict, I prefer using the word "care-front," employed by David Augsburger, as opposed to "confront." Many people involved in conflict ministry use this term because the word "confronting" may be received negatively, while "caring" is received positively. I agree with Augsburger that "together the words 'confronting' and 'caring' provide the balance of love and power that leads to effective human relationships."[2] I use the term *care-front* as an acronym that reminds me of the way in which I should approach racial or cultural conflict in the church. This mind-set should be established prior to meeting with the disputants.

Consecration

Before approaching people with the intent to correct a racial problem between members, repent of your sins and spend time with God in prayer. One of your best weapons for combating conflict is a clear conscience and a pure heart.

Adoration

Express to God your adoration for him. Prior to approaching the people in conflict, worship God in your home, in your office, or wherever you may be. Thank God for allowing you to be part of a dynamic ministry, namely, multicultural, multiracial ministry. Thank God for the members involved in this conflict and ask for his blessings during your time with the disputants.

Realistic

Be realistic when dealing with the conflicting parties. You are not called to solve every problem members have. Many times you will feel a strong desire to be the panacea for issues that are not your own. Often, the people with the best chance to solve the problem are the people who are directly involved in the conflict.

Empathetic

Identifying with and understanding the thoughts and feelings of others are important elements when care-fronting people involved in conflict. As much as possible, put yourself in the other person's shoes. Attempt to see life from his or her point of view. Such action may help people listen to you when you have to correct them. Moreover, empathizing with people, even when they are at fault, builds bridges and not barriers.

Forthright

Once you have spent time with God, thanked him for placing you in a specialized ministry, been realistic about problem solving, and applied empathy to the people involved, you are ready to "front" the individuals involved in racial conflict. Be direct and straightforward. If someone is at fault, let him or her know it. Most people will respect you if you show them their faults. They may not like it, but they will respect you. You owe it to the parties involved to be forthright.

Reconciliation

Review Scriptures that encourage reconciliation. This is one of the greatest ministries entrusted to you. View your approach to conflict as a way to bring races and cultures together. Moreover, horizontal wellness—our relationship with others—leads to vertical wellness—our relationship with God.

Order

Maintain order at all costs. Do not let the meeting get out of control, which can easily happen when emotions and tempers flare. One thing the enemy would love to see is fighting and arguing perpetuated between two Christians from different races. A disorderly meeting will lead to a disorderly outcome.

Notes

Taking notes is an important part of care-fronting. Many times you will have subsequent meetings; referring to notes from the previous meeting will be helpful. Although some have the capability to retain information, avoid memorizing exchanges between conflicting parties. Documenting words spoken in the meeting is reliable and more than sufficient.

Time

Lastly, monitor the amount of time spent with the disputants. Spending hours with people who are attempting to resolve conflict is taxing. Also, if you have more than one such incident, you could find yourself spending most of your time counseling individuals. If counseling people is not your primary call to ministry, you could easily burn out.

Pauline Example

Not only did the apostle Paul have to deal with people who had problems with other races and cultures, but he also had to care-front some of these individuals. Interfacing with people who were prejudiced was surely disheartening to the apostle. With passion, love, and obedience, however, Paul fulfilled his call to multicultural, multiracial ministry. He affirmed that God is the "God of the Gentiles" (Rom 3:29) and that God loves Gentiles (Rom 9:24-25). Likewise, Paul preached to the Gentiles (Gal 1:16) and taught them (1 Tim 2:7). He explained his calling to the Galatians: "But when he who had set me apart, even from my mother's womb, and called me through his grace, was pleased to reveal his Son in me, that I might preach him among the Gentiles, I did not immediately consult with flesh and blood" (Gal 1:16).

While defending this call, Paul wrote, "And it was because of a revelation that I went up; and I submitted to them the gospel which I preach among the Gentiles" (Gal 2:2). He also wrote, "for he who effectually worked for Peter in his apostleship to the circumcised effectually worked for me also to the Gentiles" (Gal 2:8).

Several passages reflect Paul's passion, love, and obedience to his call. To the Romans, he wrote,

> And I do not want you to be unaware, brethren, that often I have planned to come to you (and have been prevented thus far) in order that I might obtain some fruit among you also, even as among the rest of the Gentiles. I am under obligation both to Greeks and to barbarians, both to the wise and to the foolish. For I am not ashamed of the gospel, for it is the power of God for salvation to everyone who believes, to the Jew first and also to the Greek. (Rom 1:13-16)

Moreover, Paul care-fronted Jews who practiced hypocrisy when relating to Gentiles. He told the Galatians, "But when Cephas came to Antioch, I opposed him to his face, because he stood condemned. For prior to the coming of certain men from James, he used to eat with the Gentiles; but when they came, he began to withdraw and hold himself aloof, fearing the party of the circumcision. And the rest of the Jews joined him in hypocrisy" (Gal 2:11-13).

Such action shows Paul's effort to safeguard the interests of the gospel to the Gentiles. It also informs Peter that his actions are negligible and do not reflect the love of God. In that same vein, we read, "If someone says, 'I love God,' and hates his brother, he is a liar; for the one who does not love his brother whom he has seen, cannot love God whom he has not seen" (1 John 4:20).

Mediating Racial Conflict in the Church

What happens when more than two people from different races are involved in a conflict? What do you do when several representatives from, for example, the White race are in conflict with several representatives from the Black race? Sam Leonard, in *Mediation the Book*, provides a step-by-step method for mediating conflict in which several people are involved.[3] My adaptation of these methods has proved helpful in my resolving conflict among races and cultures. The methods are divided into three stages: the *pre-mediation* stage, the *mediation* stage, and the *post-mediation* stage. You can adapt these methods and use them in your context of ministry.

Pre-mediation stage

Step 1: Contact key players. In this stage of mediation, you will contact all key players and ask for one representative from each group. Be sure to collect the basic facts of the dispute. Have them explain to you what happened from their perspectives. Simultaneously, be intentional at building a relationship with the disputants. Finally, explain to the disputants the mediation process and schedule the first meeting.

Step 2: Establish a problem-solving environment. Arrange the room in a manner that will help the players feel comfortable. If you have a large group, use square tables arranged in a U-shaped formation. It is also helpful to provide tablecloths and flowers. Finally, have refreshments and coffee or tea for the participants. The goal is to have a mediation-friendly room.

Mediation stage

Step 3: Educate the disputants about mediation. The objective of this stage is for you to explain the process and establish control. You will also get the disputants to sign an agreement stating their willingness to mediate the dispute.

Step 4: Elicit perspectives. Ask the person who initiated the mediation to share his or her perspective with you. Be prepared for disputants to use this time to vent.

Step 5: Set the agenda. Set up a flip chart and list the problems. It is helpful to write down the issues as joint workable problem questions.

Step 6: Collect data needed to solve each agenda issue. For each issue, either collect the information during the meeting or assign homework. Between this meeting and the next one, the disputants can gather information they need and bring it back to the meeting in order to make an informed decision.

Step 7: Enter the problem-solving phase of mediation. Facilitate the resolution of each agenda item one by one. Assist the parties to negotiate a settlement.

Step 8: Prepare the written agreement. Finalize the terms of the settlement in a written document. By putting the settlement in writing, you honor the work of the people.

Step 9: Enter the closure phase. Meet with the parties again and present them with the final completed documents. Review for corrections.

Post-mediation stage

Step 10: Follow up. After the argument is settled, call those who were involved in the dispute and obtain an evaluation from them.

How Did Jesus Care-front a Racial Issue?

"The Samaritan woman therefore said to him, 'How is it that you being a Jew, ask me for a drink since I am a Samaritan woman?' (For Jews had no dealings with Samaritans)" (John 4:9). In the context of this Scripture passage, Jesus care-fronts barriers that divide people. One barrier involves gender and the other involves race and culture. I'll focus on the latter barrier. How Jesus handles the Samaritan woman's question provides insight for dealing with racial issues. Also, keep in mind that the Samaritan woman was not a follower of Christ at this point. Thus, Jesus' approach differs from the way he might approach a believer.

Initially, Jesus avoids addressing what could have been a negative conversation topic. Rather, he talks about the woman's need (spiritual awakening) and explains that he is able to supply the need (John 4:10). Jesus built a bridge from the secular to the spiritual with his words. He did not play the race card but gently and diplomatically put that card back in the deck. Leaders, listen carefully! Sometimes it is not beneficial to talk about racial issues with people who are not Christians. Be led by the Spirit and always have the person's spiritual welfare at heart.

II. The Beauty of Diversity

Now we will venture inside the focus group's meeting. I spent twelve weeks with a multicultural, multiracial group; we talked together about several racial and cultural issues. One of our sessions focused on understanding and comparing cultures. When diverse groups in a multicultural, multiracial church attempt to understand each other's cultures, conflict among members can be curtailed.

We sought to understand time- and event-oriented cultures, as well as cultures related to "formality" and "informality." I believe that in order to minimize conflict in an integrated church and to minister effectively in cross-cultural settings, people must understand what culture is and how culture is acquired. These two areas were discussed during the session. Moreover, the members of the diverse group confirmed that members of multicultural, multiracial churches should study and understand these areas. I began the session by supplying the group with two basic assumptions: (1) culture resembles a mental road map or a computer software packet, and (2) we are born cultureless. I adapted these assumptions from Daniel Sanchez's cultural sensitivity seminar.[4]

Understanding This Intangible Thing Called "Culture"

How can we explain and gain a better understanding of what culture is? Culture can be likened to a mental road map or a computer software packet. For example, the first time I visited my community in the Dallas, Texas, area, I needed a map to guide me. However, after several years of traveling to the same location, I developed a mental map that I now use almost unconsciously. Culture operates in a similar way. Also, one can compare culture to a computer program. For example, many people attempt to get things done on their computers only to find that the computers do not perform according to the commands they receive. After carefully searching for the problem, they find that the computers have different programs. In other words, the computers were functioning according to the programs they received. For human beings, culture is like the computer program that enables humans to function on the basis of what they know and understand. Furthermore, when one culture has difficulties understanding other cultures, it might be because they have different "computer programs." Thus, this mental map or computer program becomes the design by which individuals organize their lives, interpret their experience, and evaluate the behavior of others.

I believe we are born "cultureless"—we do not inherit culture biologically but learn it from the societies in which we live. For example, if a Russian infant were adopted by an African American family, the infant would mature with the same skills to learn the English language and customs as the African American children in the family. The cultural learning process, called "enculturation," begins immediately. It is the natural process of formal and informal, intentional and unintentional means by which children are inducted into a community and acquire its culture.

After we discussed these assumptions, I had our focus group form smaller groups in order to discuss a topic related to event-oriented versus time-oriented people and also formality and informality.

Several Races Dialogue about Cultural Distinctions and Norms

Participants were asked to respond to the following questions: Do you recognize time-oriented and event-oriented people at North Garland Baptist Fellowship? What is the cross-cultural minister to do when pastoring such individuals? These questions are important because many church members arrive at church late, and such action disturbs people from certain cultures.

The majority of the focus group recommends that the cross-cultural minister begin services on time. Member *O*, a white male, said, "It's not when you start but when you finish." The group then discussed the importance of the multicultural, multiracial pastor teaching and modeling punctuality. *E*, an African American female, believes the pastor should "periodically speak to the issue of timeliness." This led to another important factor to consider, namely, that traditionally many African American pastors remain in their offices during a vast portion of the worship service. The focus group was asked to reflect on this historical and traditional practice of African American pastors. Does such practice train members to come to church late? If such pastors are ministering to multicultural, multiracial churches, should they change their practice of coming to the pulpit sometime after the service starts?

The responses varied. *A*, a white male, said, "I think if the pastor comes out late, this will encourage others to come late. This also can imply that devotion is not important." *K*, a white male, suggested that the "pastor could be having devotion in his office." *D*, an African American male, said, "You should not change to accommodate the white community; just make sure the service starts on time." *F*, an African American female, said, "The pastor coming out late trains others to come late." Overall, the advice from this focus group is to begin worship services on time.

Another significant issue emerging from this session related to formality and informality. The group was presented with this question: Is it disrespectful to call ethnic pastors by their first names? While a majority of the white focus group members said it is not disrespectful to call pastors by their first names, most of the African Americans disagreed. It is the author's view that if an African American pastor wants to integrate his church with people who are accustomed to calling pastors by their first names, then the African American pastor ought to accept this. If white pastors are trying to integrate their churches with African Americans or other ethnic groups that are accustomed to calling pastors "Reverend," "Pastor," or "Dr.," then they ought to accept this. I say this because I have had members who addressed me as "Pastor," "Reverend," and "Tony," and over the course of my pastorate, I have experienced representatives of each group respecting and disrespecting me. If pastors experience discomfort as a result of being called by their first names, then address pastors by their titles in public and by their first names in private—with their permission, of course. Ultimately, pastors will inform you of what they desire.

Finally, if you conduct a similar seminar, consider enhancing the session by inviting people who are time-oriented and event-oriented to explain how such tendencies were acquired. I offer this suggestion because member *L*, who is from Nigeria, gave an insightful explanation as to why he is event-oriented. He wrote,

> The term "African Time" is a well known term and widely used all over the continent of Africa. This is not to disrespect the people of Africa, as to say that they keep a non-standardize time that differentiates them from the rest of the world; but rather it is to say it is customary if you want people to be on time to an event or an occasion you tell them that it is going to start one hour earlier than the real time. This is to give them a one-hour preparation period. During earlier times Africans were more of an event-oriented community rather than a time-oriented community.

If you are involved in a multicultural, multiracial ministry, you need to take various cultural aspects into consideration for the integration of the community. As each culture has its own distinctiveness, the leaders must have room for mutual appreciation and adaptation. Also, leaders must avoid imposing their cultural preferences on the members of other cultures in their worshipping community.

NOTES

[1] Joyce L. Hocker and William W. Wilmot, *Interpersonal Conflict* (Boston: McGraw Hill Companies Inc., 1998), 19.

[2] David Augsburger, *Caring Enough to Confront* (Ventura CA: Regal, 1981), 9.

[3] Sam Leonard, *Mediation: The Book* (Evanston IL: Evanston Publishing, Inc., 1994), 111.

[4] While researching the area of multicultural, multiracial ministry, Dr. Daniel Sanchez shared some of his research with me. This section on "assumptions" is adapted from his cultural sensitivity seminar. Dr. Sanchez is professor of missions at Southwestern Baptist Theological Seminary, Fort Worth, Texas.

DISCUSSION QUESTIONS

1. Identify and explain four traps to avoid when dealing with conflict in a multiracial, multicultural church. As a group, list two more traps.

2. What are nine ways to care-front racial problems in the congregation?

3. Who did the Apostle Paul rebuke because of prejudice? Where is this event described in Scripture?

4. Identify a racial conflict in which you or someone you know was involved. How was the conflict handled? What methods could have been improved?

5. Explain the difference between time-oriented and event-oriented cultures. By which do you prefer to live? Do you prefer to live by both?

CHAPTER FOUR

Surface Integration Is Not Enough

Establishing cross-cultural, cross-racial relationships takes work. Such relationships seldom happen automatically. Due to fears, doubts, anxiety, ignorance, and other reasons, people generally find it easier to develop relationships with members of their own culture and race.

In order to grow and sustain healthy, vibrant, multicultural, multiracial churches, cross-cultural relationships must be established. They cannot be limited merely to exchanging words on Sunday mornings or to giving and receiving smiles while passing each other in the church building.

I. Building Relationships

I recently attended a Dallas Mavericks versus Washington Wizards game. This was my first time seeing basketball's superstar Michael Jordan play in person. The American Airlines Arena, home of the Mavericks, was packed to capacity. People from many cultures and races attended the game. They were smiling at each other, cheering together, and even sharing popcorn. The people I met were so friendly it seemed as though I'd known them all my life. The unity and oneness I felt and saw was incredible—we were connected! At the end of the game, people got back to their normal routines. The cheering was over and most people did not have time to exchange smiles. People rushed to their vehicles and went their separate ways.

I am not suggesting that these people should have done something different. The game was over and they went home. The brief relationships established during the game will never be nurtured. In fact, we may never again see the people we met at the game. That is all right. No one should expect anything more from a group of people who attend a ballgame. However, should we expect the same behavior from people of various cultures and races who attend the same local church? Unfortunately, in some multicultural, multiracial congregations, people attend church together, sing together, pray together, and exchange smiles, but when the Sunday morning service ends, those brief relationships are not nurtured. I call this "surface integration." I do not believe people intentionally avoid building and nurturing cross-cultural relationships. I do think, however, that people generally find it easier to develop relationships with members of their own culture and race. Such tendencies should motivate us to recognize barriers that impede relationships.

Six Barriers

Several years ago, a good friend of mine, our assistant pastor at the time, brainstormed with me concerning barriers our members might encounter. Some of these barriers are subtle; others are crystal-clear. From our observations and experiences in providing pastoral care to the same integrated congregation, we created a list of potential barriers.

1. Surface integration

Surface integration occurs when members of multicultural, multiracial churches worship together on Sunday morning and are satisfied with only that experience. It is easy for people to think they have done their duty to further the multicultural, multiracial movement by worshiping with members of other races. This is simply not enough. Relationships must continue beyond the church walls.

2. Lack of communication

Another barrier that members of integrated churches encounter involves communication. Again, it is easy for one to feel comfortable at a church that different races and cultures attend without conversing with those who are racially and culturally different. An intentional effort to stretch our communicating beyond a "Hello" or a "See you next Sunday" is beneficial to this ministry. In addition, people should be aware of how they communicate. For one group to refer to another group as "you people" would probably be viewed as a racist remark. The types of phrases people use can make or break progress.

3. Different lifestyles and interests

One of the subtlest barriers that hinders healthy cross-cultural, cross-racial relationships is our lifestyles and interests. Some people who share the same ethnicity do not have anything in common. This lack of having something in common makes building relationships difficult. Imagine trying to build relationships between people who are from different ethnic backgrounds. The difficulty increases. Working with these different groups is challenging. The word "intentional" is important. Members in integrated churches must be unapologetically intentional when building relationships.

4. Busyness

Surface integration flourishes in multicultural, multiracial churches because people are too busy to establish relationships. I have heard the following comments many times: "I work twelve hours a day, so I can't come." "The kids have homework and I simply do not have time." "By the time I get finished taking the kids to their soccer and baseball games and complete all the other things I have to do on the weekend, I'm exhausted." Certainly, people are busy. I do not fault parents for spending time with their families. I do believe, however, that we can be creative amid our busy schedules and build relationships.

5. Negative experiences

One of the most candid barriers to building relationships across cultural and racial lines is a negative experience with other races and cultures. Such experiences occur within all types of racial and cultural groups. In integrated churches, people need time to trust other racial groups when they have been the victims of racism from people within that group. Certainly we should not attribute the characteristics of one person to their entire ethnic or cultural group, but it is human nature to do so.

6. Prejudice

Another barrier that impedes relationships across racial lines is the sin of prejudice. One myth concerning multicultural, multiracial churches is that all members are free from the sin of prejudice. This is not true. Many people attend such churches in order to be healed from this sin. However, for many of these people, being part of an integrated church is difficult, a fact that is sometimes evident in how they interact with other races.

Cultivating Cross-cultural, Cross-racial Relationships

Several factors are involved in cultivating healthy relationships with other races and cultures in the local church. Those who attend integrated churches have achieved the first step in the cultivating process, namely, worshiping together. There are, however, additional factors that contribute to sustained cross-cultural/racial relationships.

Working together

Doing the Lord's work with people from diverse backgrounds is rewarding. Sharing common ministerial goals almost always leads to a unique bond among those who minister. Currently, our preaching staff has representatives from the African American community, the community of India, and the White community. It is a joy spending time together planning and talking about our preaching ministry.

Crying together

Another factor that cultivates relationships is ministering to hurting people. Pain knows no color, and suffering is not prejudiced. We all experience distress in our lives at one time or another. During such times, race and culture make no difference; the person who offers kind words, a prayer, a hug, or encouragement makes a difference. Shared pain is the "glue" of multicultural, multiracial relationships.

Playing together

A few years ago, one of our deacons, who is white, asked me to attend a rodeo with his family. I thought, *I grew up in the hood, where all I saw were rats, cats, and dogs, and some of the rats were killing the cats and fighting the dogs. I'm not the type of guy who would attend a rodeo.* The entire experience was foreign to me. I did, however, attend, and I thoroughly enjoyed it. This event strengthened my relationships with this deacon and his family. Be willing to spend time together away from church and experience things outside of your cultural comfort zone.

Talking with one another

It is nearly impossible to nurture cross-racial, cross-cultural relationships without talking about challenges and successes that exist among people. Open and honest dialogue strengthens relationships. We may need time to become comfortable speaking openly with someone from a different race. Yet, in order for relationships to advance to the next level, we must include moments when people of different races and cultures look each other in the eyes and talk about similarities and differences. When you engage in such dialogue, you will learn many things about other people and about yourself.

The Mandate in Leviticus, Numbers, and Deuteronomy

That God is an advocate for multicultural, multiracial ministry radiates throughout passages in the books of Leviticus, Numbers, and Deuteronomy. Leviticus, while saturated with ceremonial and legalistic requirements for the Hebrew people, also addresses God's passion and love for the Gentiles: "The stranger who resides with you shall be to you as the native among you, and you shall love him as yourself . . . I am the LORD your God" (19:34). This verse is a complement to verse 18, "You shall not take vengeance, nor bear any grudge against the sons of your people, but you shall love your neighbor as yourself; I am the LORD." Furthermore, verse 18 is quoted several times in the New Testament (Matt 5:43; 19:19; 22:39; Mark 12:31; Luke 10:27; Rom 13:9; and Gal 5:14). These passages show clearly God's passion and concern for all cultures and races. Therefore, to treat the neighbor differently from the alien is contrary to the will of God. We must love neighbor and alien as we love ourselves.

Also, notice that Jesus exalts the command to love one's neighbor as oneself. This command is above all except the command to love God. The scribes and rabbis interpreted the term "neighbor" as applying to one's Jewish neighbor and not to those of other races. In the parable of the Good Samaritan, Jesus intentionally addressed this interpretation (Luke 10:30-37). His goal was to correct Jewish racial prejudice.

In ancient Israel, people expressed celebration and love for God through sacrificial worship. The method of expressing one's love for God is complex but essential (Num 15). In fact, haphazardly approaching God in worship could result in one's demise (Lev 10:1-2). Therefore, the people had regulations pertaining to worship. These regulations not only applied to the natives (Num 15:13), but also to the aliens. It is God's plan for all of humanity to worship him. Also, God does not prohibit people from worshiping him because of their culture or race. The Bible says, "And if an alien sojourns with you, or one who may be among you . . . and he wishes to make an offering by fire, as a soothing aroma to the LORD, just as you do, so he shall do" (Num 15:14).

Recognize from these passages that when "foreigners" or "aliens" come into God's community of faith, the congregation becomes culturally and racially diverse. Moreover, this results in worship from a multicultural, multiracial congregation. What does God think about this? God says, "As for the assembly, there shall be one statute for you and for the alien . . . a perpetual statute throughout your generations; as you are, so shall the alien be before the LORD" (Num 15:15). Finally, Deuteronomy records Moses' reaffirming God's ownership and love for all cultures and races. He writes, "[God] executes justice for the orphan and the widow, and shows his love for the alien" (Deut 10:17-19).

II. Developing Socials and Other Ministries

One of the most exciting aspects of serving in a church with a diverse membership is developing ministries. The goal of this section is to give you a brief overview of several ministries that have been beneficial in our multicultural, multiracial context. These programs are not meant to replace but to add to the many other ministries the church does.

Diversity banquets

A diversity banquet is an event that celebrates the various cultures and races represented in the local church. A team familiar with the demographics of the church should plan the banquets. The following is an example from my own experience: Our church includes representatives from Africa. We asked one of our Nigerian members if he could present historic facts about Nigeria. We also ate Nigerian food. Of course, at each diversity banquet we also have good old American hamburgers or hot dogs. These banquets give us an opportunity to learn about someone else's heritage and, simultaneously, taste their culture's food. Such a ministry is beneficial to learning about and appreciating another's culture.

Guess who's coming to dinner?

The main objective of "Guess Who's Coming to Dinner" is to link families from different racial and cultural backgrounds. Church leaders should plan the gathering. Create a sign-up sheet on which church members can check whether or not they want to be a "host" or a "guest" at the event. Once you have collected data, link the families, then call and inform each family as to who will be hosting them or who will be their guests. The guests may participate in supplying the dessert for the dinner. This is a wonderful time for adults and their children to visit each other's homes and fellowship. This ministry can occur once a quarter.

A.M.E.N. (Accountable Men of Every Nationality)

Every church should have a men's ministry (just as they should have a women's ministry). A men's ministry that consists of various races and cultures brings innumerable blessings. A.M.E.N. sessions include prayer, testimonies, and Bible study. Also allot time for planning retreats and outreach projects. Another rewarding activity is pairing up with partners and holding one another accountable in many areas, including race relations. This ministry can meet once a month at the local church.

R.A.C.E. (Race and Caring Encounters)

The Race and Caring Encounters ministry is a home cell group that fosters fellowship and bonding among members. A distinctive of this ministry is that it provides a forum where issues related to race and culture can be discussed in healthy ways. During the discussions, the emphasis is not on sharing one's opinion but on seeking answers to various questions he or she has regarding race.

DISCUSSION QUESTIONS

1. Discuss three barriers to building cross-cultural, cross-racial relationships.

2. Identify and explain factors that cultivate cross-cultural, cross-racial relationships.

3. What does God's word tell us to do in Leviticus 19:34? How is this relevant to multicultural, multiracial ministries? How does it relate to what Jesus says in the New Testament?

4. According to Numbers and Deuteronomy, explain how multicultural, multiracial ministry is seen in the heart of God.

5. Why is it important to develop ministries that meet everyone's needs in a diverse congregation? Should these ministries replace the traditional ones?

CHAPTER FIVE

Recruiting and Coaching the Dream Team

It is beneficial for the staff in a multicultural, multiracial church to reflect the congregation. When people consider joining a multicultural, multiracial church, they often wonder if the church has an integrated staff. Having such a staff is one way to show one's commitment to having this kind of ministry.

In addition, because lay leaders are not as visible as those are with a platform ministry, it is important to have representatives from different cultural and racial groups serving in various ministries. Also, the professional and lay staff are crucial when it comes to evangelizing and winning souls to Christ.

I. Hiring Staff Members

One of the best ways to communicate a goal of racial and cultural diversity is to have a diversified staff. Actions do speak louder than words. If leaders tell members they want the church to be integrated, but members do not see an effort to integrate the staff, such a claim will not be taken seriously. In addition to diversifying the staff, the lay leaders should reflect the cultural and racial profile of the congregation. With much prayer, patience, and intentionality, lay leaders should be carefully selected and mobilized into ministry. There are, however, several pitfalls to avoid.

Four Pitfalls

When I began hiring staff members and asking lay leaders to serve our congregation, I was so concerned with keeping the balance that I temporarily lost sight of our primary purpose as Christians. We are here first and foremost to worship and exalt our Lord and Savior Jesus Christ. One way to turn your multicultural, multiracial dream into a nightmare is to stray from this reality. The following are a few of my mistakes. I am thankful, however, that the lessons learned from these mistakes have returned great spiritual dividends.

1. Avoid hiring people solely on the basis of color

There was a point in my ministry when my greatest desire was to keep the racial "balance" within our leadership. I tried to accomplish this by placing laypeople into positions primarily on the basis of their profession of faith in Christ and their ethnic background. This is a huge mistake to avoid. Numerous requirements for conducting ministries have nothing to do with one's color. Do not fall into this "pit"; you will do nothing but load unnecessary pressure upon yourself.

2. Resist hiring people solely on the basis of education

I am a firm believer in education. I humbly admit that I have four earned degrees, and next year I begin working on my fifth degree—a second earned doctorate. Regardless, none of my classes during formal theological training prepared me for this specific ministry. A few of the classes addressed marginal factors that have assisted me, but none of them dealt with the core issues involved in multicultural, multiracial ministry. Thus, a person may have an earned degree in any theological field but may lack knowledge/experience required for ministry in an integrated context.

3. Avoid hiring unbelievers who taught a secular diversity class

Regarding efforts to enhance race relations, corporate America has, in many ways, shamed the local church. Although one would have a valid argument when he or she says that corporate America has been forced to face the race issue, the fact remains that the corporate world has implemented goals to ensure cultural competence among its employees. While I applaud this effort, people responsible for hiring staff members in integrated churches should not hire people solely because they taught a class on diversity in the secular world. This is especially true if the person is an unbeliever. Hiring such individuals sends the wrong message to both the congregation and the person who teaches in corporate America. The church must not compromise its standard for admitting people into membership in general and leadership in particular. That a staff member has a personal relationship with Jesus Christ ought to be the first qualification without compromise.

4. Avoid hiring people solely based on an interracial marriage

Members of interracial couples may seem like the best candidates for leadership positions in multicultural, multiracial churches. Nevertheless, we must remember that a marriage relationship involves two people—the husband and the wife. A member of a staff is in a relationship involving hundreds, and in some instances thousands, of people from various backgrounds. Leading effectively in an integrated church requires much more than marrying cross-culturally or cross-racially.

How to Select a Complementary Staff

Pastors, search committees, or personnel committees have the responsibility to select complementary staff for a multicultural, multiracial congregation. This is no small task. In fact it is one of the most challenging responsibilities of leadership in intentionally integrated churches. The key is hiring people who share the multicultural, multiracial vision. Additionally, these leaders should show promise for producing leaders who can disciple others. Consider the following factors when searching for leaders.

Scriptural competence regarding race relations

It is essential to hire individuals who have a biblical understanding of how God sees people of all colors. Although this is relatively simple, the number of Christians who believe God is a respecter of people regarding race and culture is surprising. How does God want his people to get along? Why does God love everyone? What does God's word teach about prejudice? Potential staff members should be able to answer these questions prior to getting the job.

Prior experience in multicultural, multiracial ministry

Many people have experience working in a diverse ministry context. These people are prime prospects for the staff. Some individuals of a particular race are willing to work in a context totally different from theirs. These people are rare, and most of them have already overcome many barriers to progress. Seek such people.

Former missionaries seeking to serve a church

Without exception, former missionaries are among the best people to serve in multicultural, multiracial contexts. Although they may exist, I have not met a missionary who did not have a genuine love for people regardless of their race, culture, or background. Get names of retired/former missionaries from your local associations and conventions. Some of these people desire either to work in the local church or to volunteer their services.

Students who express a calling to multicultural, multiracial ministry

Bible colleges and seminaries are full of students who feel called to serve in integrated churches. Although they may have little experience, they are wonderful candidates for training. Outstanding students whom we located at Bible colleges and seminaries have blessed our church. We posted flyers indicating our vision concerning multicultural, multiracial ministry, and we have reaped great dividends. Three of our former staff members now serve as pastors in various parts of the United States. God is working in the hearts of these students. He is breaking down barriers and calling us to oneness. Many students are not only interested in understanding racial and cultural harmony from a biblical perspective, but they also want to experience it in the life of the church.

Teachable Christians

An important qualification of a staff member is a teachable spirit. Integrated ministry is new to many people, and there is much to learn. Leaders who have paved the way are looking for people willing to listen and learn about how to serve in a diverse ministry context.

Utilizing a Search Committee

Regardless of a church's size, it is wise to use search committees to assist the pastor with hiring staff. The process is so involved that one person, particularly the pastor, does not have time to cover all bases effectively. Frank Lewis has written a book titled *The Team Builder*.[1] I have adapted part of his outline as a resource for search committees who are hiring a multicultural, multiracial staff. Any church that adapts this procedure will ensure a thorough and effective search process.

The first goal of most multicultural, multiracial churches is to hire appropriate leadership, which is best done through a search committee. I recommend no more than five people on the committee. Once the search committee is in place, have a church-wide prayer meeting specifically for locating the right person for the job. The following four steps will assist a search committee as they seek competent and complementary staff members.

Develop a profile

When necessary, the committee leads the congregation in developing a profile for the prospective staff member. The profile involves several areas:

(a) *Salvation experience*—Learn how long the candidate has been saved. Try to avoid hiring a person new to the faith.

(b) *Call to ministry*—The candidate should be able to articulate his or her call to the ministry position.

(c) S*criptural qualification*—The candidate should display characteristics consistent with biblical principles for leadership. The Pastoral Epistles offer information about the type of leader who should serve the church.

(d) *Educational and academic preparation*—Determine the minimal degree requirement for the candidate.

(e) *Ministerial experience*—There is a big difference between a person with ten years of ministerial experience in one place and a person with two years of experience in five different places. I personally do not think the latter is a hindrance, but be aware of the difference.

(f) *Gifts, passion, and spiritual disciplines*—The candidate should have a strong prayer life and should be aware of what his or her gifts are.

(g) *Cultural sensitivity*—Ensure that the candidate can work in a multicultural, multiracial ministerial context.

Begin reviewing resumes

Once the church has accepted the profile, the search committee should begin reviewing resumes. The following guidelines can be helpful for the committee.

(a) *Set a deadline* for the reception of resumes.

(b) *Pray more intensely* for the needs of the church during this phase.

(c) Think about the *vision of the church* and its future ministry and how the candidate will fit into that overall vision.

(d) As a committee, ask yourselves various questions concerning your ministry. Get strong input from church leadership.

- Where do we see ourselves in five years?
- What will a new staff member find as he or she moves to this field of ministry?
- What are the strengths of our church?
- What are the reasons a prospective staff member would want to move to this church?

(e) Understand the positive aspects for a prospective staff member, then consider the possible negatives.

Visit the candidates

After narrowing the list to three people, and depending on the budget of the church, visit the church of each candidate. Next, prioritize the list from one to three with everyone agreeing on the arrangement. Now you are ready to dialogue with the top candidate. Be ready to supply him or her with salary information, benefits, expectations, responsibilities, and opportunities. Additionally, provide the candidate with a fact folder that includes continuing education opportunities, vacation time, annuity and retirement information, human and financial resources available, and an area map with location of schools. Also, provide the candidate with a realtor's brochure showing available housing, and offer him or her a recent newspaper.

The formal interview

The formal interview could encompass an entire weekend. Again, if budgeting allows, bring the candidate's entire family to visit your area. Let the candidate meet several leadership groups within the church. Perhaps you could encourage willing church members to plan a banquet. During this weekend, the pastoral team should meet the candidate and have an opportunity to ask questions. Questions regarding multicultural, multiracial ministry should be asked by members of the church and when the pastor interviews the candidate. It is crucial to be totally honest and candid when interviewing prospective staff members. Give clear expectations and goals. It is my practice to inform candidates of what will help them progress in this ministry as well as what could cause them to be terminated. I personally believe that much of the problems pastors have with staff members could be avoided with a thorough interviewing process.

Maintaining Balance When Staff Leaves

One of the most frustrating times for pastors is when they lose a quality staff member. It is more frustrating if the staff member is from a different race or culture. What can pastors do when this occurs? How does one maintain the balance among staff members when someone leaves? First, ask laity to perform various duties the staff member performed. Several years ago, one of our white pastors was called to a church in another state. Although the church was happy for the pastor, we were still left with an empty feeling. His presence alone was vital to members and visitors who came to our church. We decided to ask white church members to read Scripture and pray. In this way we, at least, provided visibility and representation from the White race in the pulpit. Simultaneously, we reassured the congregation that we were praying and working on finding a quality replacement for the person who left. Do not hesitate to ask church members for help. They are ready and willing to serve in various capacities. Remember, however, only to use individuals who are spiritual and who love the Lord. If you do not have such people of that ethnicity in the congregation, use other God-loving people, regardless of race or culture.

Jesus Practiced Cross-cultural Ministry with His Staff

"Behold, I say to you, lift up your eyes and look on the fields, that they are white for harvest" (John 4:35). The words of our Lord are clear. He is inviting his disciples to witness cross-culturally. He says, in essence, that when they (Jews) reach out and share the good news with Samaritans, such ministry will be "food" for them. Jesus encouraged his disciples to see the great harvest in their midst. This is no surprise, for Jesus' ministry included a multicultural, multiracial emphasis. Many of his encounters with people from another culture were in the presence of his disciples and the public at large.

Preaching to various races

The first message Jesus preached in Nazareth included and embraced the Gentiles. He referred to a widow living in the land of Zarephath, in Sidon. He also mentioned Naaman the Syrian (Luke 4:16-27) in a positive way. Additionally, Jesus' public ministry demonstrated God's passion to minister cross-culturally. The healing of the Gadarene demoniac revealed such passion (Matt 8:28-34), along with the healing of the Samaritan leper (Luke 17:12-19). Jesus commended the faith of the Gentiles. He marveled at a centurion's faith: "Truly I say to you, I have not found such great faith with anyone in Israel. And I say unto you that many shall come from east and west, and recline at the table with Abraham, and Isaac, and Jacob in the kingdom of heaven" (Matt 8:10-11).

On several occasions, the Bible shows Jesus extending his love to people who are racially and culturally different. These biblical examples motivate those who work in multicultural, multiracial ministry to continue reaching out to all people. One example involves Jesus' healing of a Roman soldier's servant (Matt 8:5-13). Howard Vos writes, "This gave Him occasion to observe that though the kingdom was offered primarily to the Jews, hosts of Gentiles will participate in it."[2] The Bible also reveals that Jesus ministered to the Syrophoenician woman, a Canaanite (Mark 7).

The commissions of Christ

The commissions of Christ reveal his last words to his disciples. Jesus was crucified (John 19:18), then died (19:30) and was buried (19:42). Afterward, he rose from the dead (Matt 28:6) and appeared to his disciples throughout a forty-day period (Acts 1:3). During this period, he told the disciples what they were to do in the world: "Peace be unto you; as the Father has sent me, I also send you" (John 20:21). As God sent Jesus into the world to bring redemption to all people, Jesus sends the church into the world to proclaim that redemption to all.

Jesus also said, "Go therefore and make disciples of all the nations " (Matt 28:19). Later, he said, "and you shall be my witness both in Jerusalem, and in all Judea and Samaria, and even to the remotest part of the earth" (Acts 1:8). These commissions include "all nations," and they extend to the "uttermost parts of the earth." These passages and many others bear witness to Simeon's words concerning Jesus. He said Jesus is "a light of revelation to the Gentiles, and the glory of your people Israel" (Luke 2:32).

II. Keeping It Together

According to Melvin Steinbron, "One of the struggles every pastor faces is how he can help his people personally and directly experience the love of God."[3] Steinbron also believes there is a "God-given method by which His love could be given concretely, specifically and continually to all members."[4]

That method involves a comprehensive lay ministry—a team of laypeople who can assist the pastor with shepherding the flock. Without this important ministry, the pastor and staff might experience frustration, depression, and eventually burnout.

Mobilizing a Multicultural, Multiracial Lay Ministry

Getting people involved in ministry is challenging. Many members will only get involved if they are approached directly. Some people are content with coming to church on Sunday morning and not actively participating in ministries throughout the week. How do we involve people? First, members should have a clear understanding of their responsibility as believers. The pastor's job is to equip the saints for service (Eph 4:12). Preach and teach this truth on Sunday morning and in various Christian education classes, then establish a time to meet with new and current members on a weekly basis. The purpose of the meeting is to assess the gifts, talents, and skills of each member.

Consider my schedule as an example. Approximately four weeks after a new member joins the church, my secretary schedules a time for me to meet with that person. Current members are also called to the meeting, giving them an opportunity to get to know new members. I try to meet with at least five or six people at a time. During the meeting, the members introduce themselves, tell about their prior church ministry involvement, and express what they believe to be their gifts, talents, and skills. Additionally, I give an overview of selected ministries of the church and offer them an opportunity to ask questions regarding each ministry. Since the members have already received the gifts, talents, and assessment form, they should be ready to select a place of service before the meeting ends. My secretary forwards the names of the prospective lay workers to the lay leaders. Although the pastor begins this process, the assessment procedure is a ministry that should be delegated after it is implemented and operating successfully.

When Demographics Change in the Congregation

One fact of local church ministry is that members join and members leave for various reasons. Although I define an integrated church as one that includes a noticeable presence from at least two racially diverse groups, typically, one group numerically exceeds the other. If members from the smaller group start leaving for various reasons, panic tends to surface from members of that group. How does one encourage and calm the fears of that particular race? First, pastors can meet with the particular racial group and address their fears, letting the group know that the pastor is concerned. Second, pastors should assist them in turning their fears into action, encouraging them to evangelize within their own race or culture. Also, pastors can encourage them to bring individuals who are a part of their own culture and race to the church. Third, pastors can suggest that they initiate or participate in the church's visitation program. Indeed, I advise that the visitation teams be racially and culturally diverse. Finally, I suggest that pastors and lay leaders constantly remind their members that the Holy Spirit adds to the church.

Correcting Multicultural, Multiracial Myths

As I developed and began writing this book, I identified several myths concerning multicultural, multiracial churches. I believe that if these myths are not corrected, they can impede numerical and spiritual growth.

The myth of heritage annihilation

Some people believe that individuals who attend multicultural, multiracial churches are taught to forget their heritage. Some people assume it inappropriate to talk about and reflect on one's cultural background while attending an integrated church. To the contrary, multicultural, multiracial churches highlight, reflect on, and celebrate their members' cultural distinctions in Christ.

The myth of irresponsible tolerance

Some believe that all multicultural, multiracial churches will receive anyone into their membership without biblical accountability. They reason that, since such churches are open to all races and cultures, they must be open to all sorts of lifestyles. This is incorrect. Some multicultural, multiracial churches believe that, while people do not choose who they are culturally and racially, they do choose who they are morally. Furthermore, the Bible does not use skin color as a criterion for judgment. Many multicultural, multiracial churches hold their members accountable and seek to restore those who transgress biblical mandates.

The myth of promoting interracial relationships

Some believe that the multicultural, multiracial church seeks primarily to promote interracial relationships. While I believe there is nothing unbiblical about interracial dating and marriage, promoting such relationships is not the church's purpose. In fact, multicultural, multiracial churches inform and counsel interracial couples about cultural differences that exist among them. The most important element for these churches is that relationships are biblical.

The myth of "prejudice-free" members

One of the most common myths of the multicultural, multiracial church is that the members do not harbor prejudice. Many people believe that the only way to join an integrated church is to be free from the sin of prejudice. It is true that a good number of people who attend integrated and homogeneous churches struggle with prejudice. However, being a part of an integrated church may assist in exposing one's prejudice. This can be a positive experience if individuals, once they realize their prejudice, seek to rid themselves of such attitudes.

The myth of control

Another myth concerning multicultural, multiracial churches involves white people. Some people believe that if whites are a part of the church, the style of the services in terms of music, preaching, and the like are "white-centered." This myth seems to circulate among African Americans. Additionally, many races believe that if whites are part of the multicultural, multiracial church, they must "run" or "control" how everything operates.

Similarly, others say that whites will not accept and follow the leadership of an African American pastor. In many instances, this is a myth. I witness whites following, supporting, and encouraging African American pastors and leaders regularly. Whites, along with everyone else, do not mind following leadership if the leaders exhibit integrity and competence.

The myth of "Black Standard Time"

I frequently communicate with people who believe that a church with African American members must start and end services late. This myth, based on my experience, emerges primarily from the white community. Often, when I invite whites to North Garland Baptist Fellowship, they ask whether "we start on time and if the services will last all day." Although there are many African Americans who start and end services late, there are also African Americans who are punctual and "time-oriented."

NOTES

[1] Frank Lewis, *The Team Builder* (Nashville: Convention Press, 1998), 129.

[2] Howard F. Vos, *Matthew*, Bible Study Commentary (Grand Rapids: Zondervan, 1979), 70. Also, Vos believes that this Roman soldier initiated the friendship with the Jews and was instrumental in the construction of the Capernaum synagogue.

[3] Melvon J. Steinbron, *Can the Pastor Do It Alone?* (Ventura CA: Regal Books, 1987), 25.

[4] Ibid., 26.

DISCUSSION QUESTIONS

1. Why is it important to form a search committee when hiring staff for a multicultural, multiracial church?

2. What additional steps can you add to the search process mentioned in this book?

3. List five Scriptures that show Jesus ministering cross-culturally. Discuss the passages.

4. How do the commissions of Christ involve multicultural, multiracial ministry?

5. Discuss the myths in a multicultural, multiracial church. Discuss other myths you have heard about integrated churches.

CHAPTER SIX

Confronting the "They Don't Do It Like Us" Syndrome

Unfortunately, we live in a world where we evaluate the behavior of other cultural groups by the standards of our own culture. Several years ago, I remember two of our members approaching me concerning their wedding. He was from Africa and his fiancée was American. We reviewed the details of the wedding and everyone was comfortable until I learned how long the groom wanted the ceremony to last. I remember saying, "A couple of days? I never heard of a wedding lasting a couple of days." My African friend explained to me that in his country it is not unusual for the wedding ceremony to last an entire weekend. I found this both interesting and enlightening. At that point in my ministry, and to my disappointment, I was not ready to consider a two-day event. Reflecting back on the planning of this event, there were many things I could have done to accommodate the

groom. However, thinking I had to be at the entire ceremony and being unfamiliar with the groom's wedding customs, I did not extend the ceremony. In fact, my ethnocentrism got the best of me; the wedding lasted forty-five minutes. Knowing the nature and causes of ethnocentrism can help us combat its effects on our fellow brothers and sisters in Christ.

I. Defining Ethnocentrism

A major barrier that impedes growth in multicultural, multiracial churches is known as "ethnocentrism,"[1] the tendency to view the norms and values of one's own culture as absolute and to use them as a standard against which to judge and measure all other cultures. Many times this tendency is cloaked under the attitude that "they don't do it like us." Pastors and leaders will constantly battle this area. However, the more you talk about the problems of ethnocentrism, the more your members will attempt to delete it from their attitudes.

What's Wrong with Being Ethnocentric?

While working on my doctorate, I had the privilege of researching the topic of ethnocentrism. Dr. Daniel Sanchez, Professor of Missions at Southwestern Baptist Theological Seminary, was extremely helpful.[2] He conducted a seminar on cultural sensitivity; the information in this section is adapted from his seminar. What's wrong with being ethnocentric? The answer is simple: it dishonors God because God is the creator of us all.

How do we become ethnocentric?

We become ethnocentric in many ways. First, we accept the stereotypes given to us because of our racial or cultural group. Time and time again, people are victims of stereotyping. Second, we avoid contact with people of other cultural or racial groups. Third, we allow pride to rule our lives. I once heard a preacher say that the key cause of pride is in the middle of the word *pride*. What is in the middle of the word *pride*? The letter "I." Finally, many of us have a psychological need to look down on other people. This is part of the fall of humanity. I am thankful, however, that there are ways we can overcome ethnocentrism.

Four ways to overcome ethnocentrism

In order to overcome ethnocentrism, we must first recognize that all of us have the tendency to be ethnocentric. Next, we must repent of the sin of pride.

Third, we should resolve to cultivate a friendship with at least one person of a different racial or cultural group. Fourth, we should resist efforts on the part of people in our cultural group to put down or perpetuate negative stereotypes (through jokes and snide remarks) of another cultural group. Lastly, we overcome ethnocentrism by realizing that we have an opportunity to exert a positive Christian influence in building bridges between cultural groups.

Let's get our "act" together

It is time for Christians to get our act together. We can make a positive influence on the world in which we live if we combat ethnocentrism effectively. Christians in the book of Acts certainly had their act together. According to Acts, Christianity reaches several racial and ethnic groups, which supports the claim that God embraces multicultural, multiracial ministry. For example, Philip preaches to an Ethiopian eunuch (Acts 8:35) and baptizes him (Acts 8:38). Additionally, Peter preaches to Cornelius, a Gentile soldier. Peter says, "You yourselves know how unlawful it is for a man who is a Jew to associate with a foreigner or to visit him; and yet God has shown me that I should not call any man unholy or unclean" (Acts 10:28).

Acts reveals the Jews at the church in Antioch delivering their message to the Greeks (Acts 11:20). Names and homelands point to cultural and racial diversity among the leadership at the church in Antioch (Acts 13:1). Moreover, the Holy Spirit leads this multicultural, multiracial body of leaders to commission the Apostle Paul and Barnabas (Acts 13:3). Afterward, Paul and Barnabas proclaim the gospel to a diverse group of people on an island (Acts 13:4). Egyptians, Phoenicians, Greeks, Assyrians, and Persians colonized this island.

II. Avoiding Stereotypes

Recall the focus group with whom I worked for several weeks. (See chapter 1 to review their profiles.) The group consists of members at the church I currently pastor. Each person was an enormous help as I researched how stereotypes function.

Observing Stereotypical Behavior within an Integrated Focus Group

While I met with this integrated group, one major activity involved an exercise in which seven focus group members took turns wearing labeled hats.

The people wearing the hats did not know what their own labels said, though everyone else could see them.

The objective of this exercise was to have those wearing hats identify their labels based on how other group members reacted. Prior to wearing the hats, no one in the group knew what labels were in the mix. Additionally, discarding hats after members wore them prevented repetition. The labels were inner-city African American, Southern Anglo female, Chinese American male on welfare, Mexican American, average Anglo male, suburban African American, and Native American.

I assigned three focus members to observe and evaluate the interaction among these who wore the hats and those who supplied information. They were asked to examine body language, facial expressions, tones of voice, and the like. They also recorded the time it took for each of the hat wearers to guess whose hat they wore.

One significant part of this session involves evaluators reporting observations to the focus group. The hat exercise reveals the difficulty of avoiding stereotypes when encountering cultures and races other than one's own. To distinguish between each participant, the term "observer" refers to the evaluator, the term "receiver" refers to the person wearing the hat, and the term "sender" refers to the person supplying the information. The letters assigned to focus group members below represent the same members in the profile.

Mexican American

The first volunteer, receiver *B*, a white male, picked the hat with the label "Mexican American." He was immediately addressed by one of the senders in Spanish. Assuming that all Mexican Americans speak Spanish was the predominate stereotype recorded by observers. All participants believe it is important to remember that not all Mexican Americans are fluent in Spanish. For example, some of the focus group members who are not Hispanic claim that they speak better Spanish than some of their Mexican American friends. The group found this point helpful. They all agreed that they would attempt to avoid using stereotypes while going through the exercise.

Average Anglo male

Receiver *L*, from Nigeria, picked the hat labeled "average Anglo male." The entire group laughed when he placed the hat on his head. Senders talked about drinking coffee, and many senders mentioned playing golf. At the conclusion of the segment, the group agreed on the predominate stereotype that all white men play golf.[3]

Native American

Receiver *A*, a white male, picked the hat labeled "Native American." One of the senders gave the receiver historical facts about treaties. The receiver immediately guessed who he was. All the observers said this was stereotypical and could be insulting. Focus group member *C*, a white female, asked, "Would we address a Native American in such a way if we were holding a normal conversation with them?" This led the members to ask questions pertaining to other stereotypes of Native Americans. This interested the focus group because North Garland Baptist Fellowship has at least one Native American member who ministers to other Native Americans. It was noted that one would never know that the above-mentioned person was a Native American unless she told you.

Chinese Amcerican male on welfare

Receiver *E*, an African American female, picked the hat labeled "Chinese American male on welfare." First, after many clues from the senders, the receiver figured out that she was Chinese. When she discovered she needed money, she exclaimed, "I need financial assistance?" Two of the observers noted *E*'s surprise that Asians can need financial assistance. Sender *K* remarked, "Asian Americans are hard workers, and the ones that come to the United States are the cream of the crop. Therefore, it would be assumed that they are not on welfare."

Suburban African American

Receiver *K*, a white male, picked the hat with the label "suburban African American." This was perhaps the most interesting one of all. Clues ranged from comments related to driving BMWs to questions like "Has anyone in the neighborhood given you problems?" Sender *I*, a white female, asked, "Why did you move away from the city?" This is interesting because many white people have moved from the city to the suburbs, and it was assumed that this suburban African American did so as well. The receiver, trying to figure out who he was, replied, "I must be bigoted, or I don't want to be around certain people." Sender *J*, an African American male, said to the receiver, "There is another brother in the neighborhood. Would you like to get together?" At this point receiver *K* figured out who he was. One of the observers stated, "White people normally don't use the term 'brother' when talking to each other, so using this language helped receiver *K* identify who he was."

Inner-city African American

Receiver *G*, a white male over 55, picked the hat labeled "inner-city African American." Sender *E* said to him, "Yo, yo my brother." Within four seconds, receiver *G* said, "I'm a black male in the hood." Everyone laughed. All observers pointed out that sender *E*'s body language, slang, and intonations were vital clues.

Southern Anglo female

Receiver *J*, an African American male, picked the hat labeled "Southern Anglo female." After brief conversations with two senders, receiver *J* figured out who he was. The observers agree that the accents employed by the senders assisted greatly. They concluded that people should not assume that all Southerners speak with such distinct accents.

Recorded time

The following list details the amount of time each receiver required to identify his or her label:

LABEL	TIME
Inner-city African American	4 seconds
Native American	5 seconds
Southern Anglo female	25 seconds
Mexican American	30 seconds
Average Anglo male	1 minute, 15 seconds
Chinese American male	2 minutes
Suburban African American	2 minutes, 30 seconds

I offer the following conclusion concerning the inner-city African American and the suburban African American. I chose these groups because of the extreme time disparity shown above. Many people have similar perceptions of how "inner-city" African Americans behave and communicate. I believe part of the problem is that these perceptions are formed by the media's depiction of this group. Using intonations and body language to identify cultural and racial groups is inadequate. Also, there is not a consistent perception of a suburban African American, perhaps due to the lack of this profile in the media. Overall, avoiding stereotyping is difficult because such practice is ingrained in our culture.

Concluding thoughts from the focus group

At the conclusion of this exercise, I asked focus group members to indicate in writing how this exercise helped them relate to people in a multicultural, multiracial church. Member *C*, a white female, stated that it is essential to "look at a person's condition as it relates to important things like salvation and not at physical and stereotypical features—don't make assumptions." She concluded her statement, "Easier said than done."

Member *J*, an African American male, wrote, "This exercise serves as a reminder that we are ministering to a multicultural, multiracial church and that we must be very careful regarding stereotyping in our conversations." Finally, member *K* stated, "We need to be sensitive to all people in our church and have an awareness of different backgrounds and cultures."

Critique of methodology

The group exercise involving labeled hats is quite effective. However, I offer this suggestion for those who might use the exercise. Try giving every focus group member an opportunity to wear a hat, alternating observers. This adjustment gives everyone an opportunity both to observe and to evaluate. Second, be intentional when choosing the hat for each participant to insure that everyone experiences, at least temporarily, immersion into another culture and race. Although this process will take more time, the participants' willingness to alternate and participate should supersede time constraints.

NOTES

[1] "Anthropologists and historians make a crucial distinction between racism on the one hand, and tribalism or ethnocentrism on the other. While racism refers to the hierarchal ranking of human beings based on biological characteristics, tribalism and ethnocentrism are nothing more than an intense preference for one's own group over strangers. Ethnocentrism comes from the Greek word *ethnos* which means 'people' or 'nation.' Ethnic groups are usually related by blood, kinship, or a common history, but these ties do not have to be racial—frequently they are not. Nationality, religion, shared traditions, and mere geographical proximity are much more common denominators for tribalism and ethnocentrism than is race. While racism is necessarily rooted in biology, ethnocentrism is typically rooted in culture" ("Ethnocentrism Versus Racism," Dinesh D'Souza, *The End Of Racism* [New York: The Free Press, 1995], 32-34).

[2] While researching the area of "ethnocentrism," Dr. Daniel Sanchez shared some of his research with me. This section on "ethnocentrism" is adapted from his cultural sensitivity seminar. Dr. Sanchez is professor of missions at Southwestern Baptist Theological Seminary, Fort Worth, Texas.

[3] During one of the seminar sessions, member *G*, the white male, said, "I have a comment. I hear many people throwing this word 'Anglo' around. What is an Anglo? I, as only a third-generation Swedish American, wonder about being called an Anglo. I don't find it insulting. Perhaps it is a misunderstanding. However, to set the record straight, I'm really not an Anglo." This interested me for several reasons, the most obvious being that I had used the term "Anglo" in the first two seminar sessions. Was member *G* indeed insulted, although he said he was not? What is the prevailing term for this class of people whom I've called "Anglo" throughout the session?

These questions led me to further research. The following day I contacted the United States Census Bureau in Dallas, Texas, and spoke with one of their representatives. I asked, "What is the appropriate term to use when referring to White America? Do you use the term Anglo, White, Caucasian, or White Caucasian?" The representative referred me to a contact at the United States Census Bureau in Silver Springs, Maryland. The contact in the Maryland office told me that the word the United States Census Bureau uses is "White."

The contact person then directed me to a web site containing categories and definitions of race and ethnicity. The categories in this classification are sociopolitical constructs and should not be interpreted as being scientific or anthropological in nature. The web site also uses "White" to refer to people having origins in any of the original peoples of Europe, the Middle East, or North Africa (see *Standards for Maintaining, Collecting, and Presenting Federal Data on Race and Ethnicity* <www.census.gov/population/www/socdemo/race/Ombdir15.html>, 21 February 2000).

Also, Europe can be divided into five geographical regions, one being Scandinavia, which includes Sweden (see *Columbia Encyclopedia*, 5th ed., s.v. "Europe"). As to the term "Anglo," Appleby writes, "Webster says an 'Anglo' would be 'a Caucasian inhabitant of the United States of non-Latin extraction.' With this in mind it is wrong to refer to most English-speaking congregations as 'Anglo'" (Jerry Appleby, *The Church Is in a Stew* [Kansas City: Beacon Hill Press, 1990], 18). This is significant because focus group member *G* stated that he was not an Anglo but rather a third-generation Swedish American. This research led me to use the term "white" during subsequent sessions.

DISCUSSION QUESTIONS

1. What is a definition of "ethnocentrism"?

2. List the four causes of ethnocentrism and discuss them. Also, list three additional causes of this tendency.

3. Discuss ways in which we can overcome ethnocentrism.

4. Do you find yourself, at times, stereotyping others? How can you overcome this problem?

5. Discuss how the book of Acts reveals the multicultural, multiracial motif.

CHAPTER SEVEN

How to Scratch Itches Through the Worship Service

Planning worship services for integrated churches is both rewarding and challenging—rewarding because nothing compares to people from different races and cultures worshiping our Lord Jesus Christ, and challenging because people are different and they bring certain expectations to the multicultural, multiracial worship service. Such expectations exist because most people come from homogeneous church settings and they are accustomed to seeing things done in a particular way or in a particular style. Ministering to people with different worship styles requires intentional planning and much prayer.

I. Different Worship Styles

As it relates to the worship service, the practical discipline of pastoral leadership is paramount in multicultural, multiracial churches. Providing leadership, care, vision, direction, and motivation in the multicultural, multiracial context are tasks the leadership undertakes. To the casual observer, such leadership seems simple, but the careful analyst recognizes the complexities involved when planning worship services for a diverse congregation. People are different, and they come from cultures with distinct beliefs and values. Such cultures, according to Eric Law, are neither good nor bad; they are simply different.[1]

I believe different types of people bring an *ecclesiastical ethnocentrism* to the multicultural, multiracial worship service. This happens because most people come from homogeneous churches in which worship has been done in a particular way or in a particular style. A keen leader recognizes the impossibility of satisfying every worship need according to one's cultural or racial persuasion. On the contrary, it is the task of leadership to embrace a theology of worship whose approach deals with the common responsibilities of Christians. One of the primary responsibilities of the church is to love and worship God (Matt 22:37). Jesus tells people to worship God in spirit and in truth (John 4:24). Furthermore, the early church met regularly to worship God (Acts 2:43-47), and believers were encouraged not to neglect assembling themselves together for worship (Heb 10:25).

Although the mandate is clear as it pertains to worship, there are still many challenges when diverse cultures and races worship together. To amplify this point, I invite you to observe the focus group members again. I will relate one of the most exciting experiences I had with this diverse group of people.

II. Seeing Worship in Black and White

One of my goals was to equip the focus group to plan worship services for multicultural, multiracial congregations. To accomplish this, we visited two traditional churches—one African American and one White—for a firsthand look at how traditional churches worship. Two weeks prior to our visit, I contacted several churches in the area. I specifically asked about the racial and cultural profiles of the churches. I wanted to know what time services began and ended, the type of songs the congregation sang, and the atmosphere of the worship services. The secretary at the White church said they are "traditional, punctual, reserved, and quiet." She also said, "You hear an amen every now and then, but we are spiritual." The secretary at the African American church, when asked what time the service dismissed, replied, "Whenever the Spirit lets us out." These two churches were distinct. They differed in terms of worship and preaching styles, cultural and racial profiles, and the length of services.

On the morning of the visits, some focus group members met at North Garland Baptist Fellowship, our home church, and rode together, while others drove directly to the churches. Prior to entering the churches, I instructed the members not to discuss their thoughts with anyone until the evening session. The focus group went to the churches unannounced and intentionally entered the sanctuaries in groups of twos and threes. This would provide some level of discretion. It also would prevent undesired speculation on the part of the pastors and members. Moreover, I did not want the pastors and members of the churches to think the focus group was a search committee. Such thoughts could have hindered the objective of the visits.

After the visits, we returned that evening to discuss our experiences. This discussion lasted nearly four hours—two hours beyond the scheduled time. I began the session by handing out a form containing the following questions:

1. How are the churches similar to and different from North Garland Baptist Fellowship?
2. What were distinguishing features of the churches?
3. What did you like and dislike about the churches?
4. If you could add something to North Garland Baptist Fellowship from either of the two churches, what would it be?

After everyone answered the questions, I asked them to talk about general observations. Due to the overwhelming responses by members of the focus group, I have arranged these observations in the following manner: white members' response to the Black church, black members' response to the White church, white members' response to the White church, and black members' response to the Black church. I list the most discussed observations.

The Black church: the White response

Most of the white focus group members believed the African American worship service was "too loud and too long." Additionally, several did not agree with the pastor's method of extending the invitation, feeling that his method reflected coercion. Some talked about their inability to understand the message due to the way it was structured and delivered. Others felt the pastor was putting on a show. However, nearly all focus group members loved the music and the visible involvement of the members in worship. Member *H* said, "They're not afraid to praise the Lord." Another white focus group member said he loves the sound and beat of the music. Member *K* commented, "The congregation has a lot of energy."

Reference was also made to the emotional atmosphere of the worship service. Most of the white members were not accustomed to worshiping in such an environment. Member *I* said, "I was taught that you don't clap your hands in church, nor do you sway back and forth. I wanted to do these things but was restrained, due to my upbringing." Member *B* said, "I didn't understand any part of the message at all." However, later in the session, *B* said, "When I was listening to the sermon, I wanted to get up and just run and shout like everyone else." *B* felt this way when the pastor began his rhythmical climax, a style unique to many African American pastors.

The White church: the Black response

Nearly all African Americans in the group enjoyed the worship service at the White church. However, member *N* felt that they sang from the hymnal too much. Member *F* said, "The invitation was almost non-existent." Member *P* said she did not like ushers skipping her during the offering. She wanted to put the visitor's card in the plate, as instructed by the pulpit, but was passed over. She raised the question, "Do they really want African Americans there?" Nonetheless, the African Americans believed the church was friendly and punctual, and that the pastor delivered a clear message. Additionally, member *E* said, "I like how the pastor came out and greeted the visitors." Member *J* said, "I like how the deacons participated in the devotional service."

The White church: the White response

Nearly all of the white focus group members said the church is friendly. Most referred to the robes worn by choir members, and nearly everyone noticed the senior citizens in the congregation. The white members were fond of the pastor because they perceived him to be friendly. They also liked his sermon. In fact, focus group member *I* said, "The sermon had three points along with an introduction, body, and a conclusion." She also made reference to the "soft amens."

I then offered an observation about the pastor that related to formality and informality. The cover of the church bulletin referred to him as "Doctor." However, the order of service referred to him as "Brother." Member *C* said, "The pastor was called by his first name by one of the other pastors." The white members like the informality.

The white members also discussed a prayer one of the deacons offered during the service. The deacon referred to a "black brother" who associates with him at work. He prayed for him and asked everyone to do the same. Although one cannot be certain either way, the focus group discussed whether or not he would have prayed that prayer if there had been no African Americans in the church. In fact, the African Americans in the focus group were the only African Americans there.

Another issue the white members addressed was the issue of "over friendliness." Some of the white members said they were embarrassed because the members at the White church tried hard—perhaps too hard—to be friendly. One White focus group member, commenting on a white usher at the church, said, "One of their members skipped right over me and shook *I*'s [an African American] hand and did not shake mine." Member *N*, an African American, replied, "Yes, one of their members greeted me several times."

One white member in the focus group wondered if the level of friendliness could be a "turn-off" for African Americans. She believes bringing such "liberal attention" to members of a particular race or culture could cause the church to lose them. I call this a "strange paradox"—losing a potential friend because one is friendly to the potential friend. I have spoken with several African Americans regarding this situation. They told me they left the White church because too much attention was given to them, and they felt it was because of their racial and cultural backgrounds.

The Black church: the Black response

Several African Americans objected to some of the words used by the pastor during the sermon. Member *J* said, "The pulpit is undisciplined, and the pastor should not prolong the service." Some did not like his "animation." Others said the worship service was too loud, while a few believed some of the songs were too lengthy. Also, the pastor's method of extending the invitation came under scrutiny. Member *F* said, "The call to Christ seems to be about adding numbers versus individuals' desire to come to Christ."

Positive observations involved the music ministry. Everyone loved the music. One focus group member said, "I like the instruments they use." Another member said, "I like the pastor's openness to share." In addition, most think the church is friendly. Furthermore, a significant number of African Americans, referring to the pastor's sermon, said they understood the message. Members *D* and *E* said one had to listen hard for the points, but they were in the message. In fact, Member *D* presented sermon notes with the points on them. He described the sermon as "a clear presentation of the gospel."

Critique of methodology

Two primary critiques relate to the methods used for this learning experience. First, when conducting this exercise in the future, I will visit one church one week and the other church the next week. This will be done in order to visit the 11:00 A.M. services at both churches. Also, I will record on videotape the service at the multicultural, multiracial church and view it the evening prior to dialogue. This allows for a complete comparison of all three distinct congregations.

Second, I recommend that participants attend the churches without friends, and if possible, without family members. This insures the absence of intentional or unintentional influences upon the thoughts of participants. I believe that, since this exercise is conducted for the purpose of observing, comparing, evaluating, and analyzing the worship styles of different cultures and races, it is beneficial to use participants who have been exposed to previous sessions regarding multicultural, multiracial ministry. Such exposure allows the participants to bring a high level of cultural competence and sensitivity to the experiment.

Moreover, if other members discover that they can attend the worship services, they may attend in large numbers. This could undermine the objectives of the exercise. Such a mishap did not confront the focus group. However, the potential for it was present.

NOTE

[1] Eric Law, *The Wold Shall Dwell with the Lamb: A Spirituality for Leadership in a Multicultural Community* (St. Louis: Chalice Press, 1993), 4.

DISCUSSION QUESTIONS

1. What would we have to change in our church to accommodate people of different races or cultures?

2. What does it mean to worship in spirit and truth?

3. What is the first and greatest commandment? Discuss how this commandment can be realized in the context of worship.

4. Do you think different races should worship together? What are the pros and cons of such worship?

CHAPTER EIGHT

Conclusion

The goal of this book has been to show the importance of multicultural, multiracial ministry. The outlook of many congregations in the United States and around the world is fast becoming more multicultural, more multiracial. We have seen that such an outlook, on the one hand, is welcomed, and, on the other hand, demands a constant learning and evaluation process within the congregation. This process helps avoid developing "cold feet" in relationships, explores common denominators for fostering multicultural, multiracial relationships, and identifies the common mistakes that are made in such congregations. It will also help the congregation to develop deeper relationships rather than just surface integration among the diverse people within the church. We have also explored proper biblical, theological, and sociological reflections on this topic. Such exploration drives us to opt for this ministry and such reflection also provides us with the required tools for it.

Though multicultural, multiracial ministry looks attractive theoretically, it certainly involves difficult stages. Therefore, another goal of this book has been to encourage leaders to identify members in their congregations who have a similar vision and a desire to work with and build relationships across racial and cultural lines. The life and growth of the congregation are, after all, *relationships*, first vertically with God and horizontally with one another!

A final word of encouragement: those who are involved in this challenging ministry must not be discouraged for not seeing immediate results nor be disturbed over initial failures. They are bound to happen. The motivating factor in this ministry is "Christ did it" and therefore we can and must do it! If at times you find yourself becoming discouraged while serving in this ministry, reflect on the following words of the Apostle John: "After these things I looked, and behold a great multitude, which no one could count, from every nation and all tribe and peoples and tongues standing before the throne and the Lamb . . ." (Rev. 7:9). How great it is to foretaste here on earth what we will see in the presence of the Lord one day in heaven. Let this be your motivating factor for ensuring that there's more than one color in your pew!

Bibliography

BOOKS

Appleby, Jerry L. *Missions Have Come Home to America: The Church's Cross-Cultural Ministry to Ethnics.* Kansas City MO: Beacon Hill Press, 1986.

——. *The Church Is in A Stew.* Kansas City MO: Beacon Hill Press, 1990.

Augsburger, David W. *Conflict Mediation Across Cultures: Pathways and Patterns.* Louisville KY: Westminister/John Knox Press, 1992.

——. *Pastoral Counseling Across Cultures.* Philadelphia PA: Westminister Press, 1986.

Brister, C. W. *Pastoral Care in the Church.* New York: HarperCollins Publishers, 1992.

Brekenridge, James, and Lillian Brekenridge. *What Color Is Your God?* Wheaton IL: Bridgepoint Books, 1995.

Bruce, F. F. *The Book of Acts.* Grand Rapids: Eerdmans Publishing, 1988.

Chaney, Charles L. *Church Planting at End of the 20th Century.* Wheaton IL: Tyndale House, 1982.

Covey, Steven. *The Seven Habits of Highly Effective People.* New York: Simon and Schuster, 1989.

Erickson, Millard. *Christian Theology.* Grand Rapids: Baker Books, 1985.

Evans, Anthony T. *Let's Get to Know Each Other: What White Christians Need to Know About Black Christians.* Nashville: Thomas Nelson Publishers, 1995.

Finzel, Hans. *The Top Ten Mistakes Leaders Make*. Wheaton: Victor Books, 1994.

Fitzpatrick, Joseph P. *One Church, Many Cultures: The Challenge of Diversity*. Kansas City MO: Sheed and Ward, 1987.

Garrett, James Leo. *Systematic Theology: Biblical, Historical and Evangelical*, volume 2. Grand Rapids: Eerdmans, 1995.

Goerner, Connor, *All Nations in God's Purpose*. Nashville: Broadman Press, 1979.

Hesselgrave, David J. *Counseling Cross-Culturally: An Introduction to Theory & Practice for Christians*. Baker Book House, 1984.

———. *Communicating Christ Cross-Culturally*. Grand Rapids: Zondervan, 1978.

———. *Planting Churches Cross-Culturally*. Grand Rapids: Baker, 1980.

Hispanic Task Force of the Baptist General Convention of Texas. *Vision 2000: Winning Hispanics for Christ*. Goals and Recommendations 1992–2000. Baptist General Convention of Texas, 1992.

Hopler, Thom, and Marcia Hopler. *Reaching the World Next Door: How to Spread the Gospel in the Midst of Many Cultures*. Downers Grove IL: InterVarsity Press, 1993.

Hunt, Boyd. *Redeemed! Eschatological Redemption and the Kingdom of God*. Grand Rapids: Broadman and Holman Publishers, 1993.

International Students, Inc. *A Movement of God's People: Changed Hearts, Changing Lives, Changing Nations*. Colorado Springs: ISI, 1993.

Jo, Euntae. *Korean-Americans and Church Growth*. Seoul Korea: Cross-Cultural Ministries Institute, 1994.

June, Lee N. *The Black Family: Past, Present and Future*. Grand Rapids: Zondervan, 1991.

Jupp, James, editor. *The Challenge of Diversity: Policy Options for a Multicultural Society*. New York: Australian Government Publishing Service, 1990.

Kaiser, Walter, C. *Genesis Exodus, Leviticus, Numbers*. Expositor's Bible Commentary. Volume 2. Edited by Frank E. Gaebelein. Grand Rapids: Zondervan, 1990.

Law, Eric. *The Wolf Shall Dwell with the Lamb: A Spirituality for Leadership in a Multicultural Community*. St. Louis: Chalice Press, 1993.

MacGorman, J. W. *Acts: The Gospel for All People*. Nashville: Broadman Press, 1992.

McIntosh, Gary and Samuel Rima. *Overcoming the Dark Side of Leadership*. Grand Rapids: Baker Books, 1989.

Morgan, Campbell G. *The Great Physician*. New York: Fleming H. Revell, 1937.

Morris, Leon. *The Gospel According to John*. New International Commentary on the New Testament. Grand Rapids: Eerdmans Publishing, 1971.

Novak, Michael. *The Rise of the Unmeltable Ethnics*. New York: MacMillan, 1972.

Ortiz, Manuel. *One New People: Models for Developing a Multiethnic Church*. Downers Grove IL: InterVarsity Press, 1996.

———. *The Hispanic Challenge: Opportunities for Confronting the Church*. Downers Grove IL: InterVarsity Press, 1993.

Packer, J. I. *God's Words*. Grand Rapids: Baker Book House, 1981.

Parnell, William. *The Coming Race Wars: A Cry for Reconciliation*. Grand Rapids: Zondervan, 1993.

Pederson, Paul. *A Handbook for Developing Multicultural Awareness.* Alexandria VA: American Association for Counseling and Development, 1988.

Perkins, Spencer, and Chris Rice. *More Than Equals.* Downers Grove: InterVarsity Press, 1993.

Polhill, John B. *Acts.* New American Commentary. Nashville: Broadman Press, 1992.

Robertson, A. T. *Word Pictures in the New Testament.* Volume 5. Fourth Gospel and the Epistles to the Hebrews. Nashville: Broadman Press, 1932.

Romano, Dugan. *Intercultural Marriage: Promises and Pitfalls.* Yarmouth ME: Intercultural Press, 1988.

Schaller, Lyle E., editor. *Center City Churches: The New Urban Frontier.* Nashville: Abingdon Press, 1993.

Steinbron, Melvon, J. *Can the Pastor Do It Alone?.* Ventura CA: Regal Books, 1981.

Thornstorm, Stephen. *Harvard Encyclopedia of American Ethnic Groups.* Cambridge: Harvard University, Balknap Press, 1980.

Van Beek, Aart. *Cross-Cultural Counseling.* Minneapolis MN: Fortress Press, 1996.

Vos, Howard. *Matthew.* Bible Study Commentary. Grand Rapids: Zondervan, 1979.

Washington, Raleigh, and Glen Kehrein. *Breaking Down Walls: A Model for Reconciliation in an Age of Racial Strife.* Chicago: Moody Press, 1993.

Wuest, Kenneth. *Word Studies from the Greek New Testament.* Volume 2. Grand Rapids: Eerdmans Publishing, 1973.

Young, Kenneth N. *A Training Program for White Professional Counselors and Ministers who have a desire to overcome the effects of racism and minister more effectively to the black community.* Portland OR: Theological Research Exchange Network, 1991.

Youngblood, Ronald, F. *Exodus.* Everyman's Bible Commentary. Chicago: Moody Bible Institute, 1983.

JOURNALS

Acosta, Sam, Lucille S. Groh, Gustavo Hernandez, and Barbara Rathbone. "Counseling Hispanics in the United States.*" Journal of Pastoral Care* 44 (spring 1990): 33-41.

Augsburger, David W. "Cross-cultural Pastoral Psychotherapy." *Clinical Handbook of Pastoral Counseling.* Volume 2: 129-43.

———. "Multicultural Pastoral Care and Counseling." *Journal of Pastoral Care* 46 (summer 1992): 103-73.

Azar, Thomas Paul. "Cross Cultural Counseling.*" Military Chaplains' Review* (fall 1990): 95-99.

Boyd, Marsha Foster. "The African American Church as a Healing Community: Theological and Psychological Dimensions of Pastoral Care." *Journal of Theology* (United Theological Seminary) 95 (1991): 15-31.

Bryant, Cullene. "Pastoral Care and Counseling in a Cross-Cultural Context: The Issue of Authority.*" Journal of Pastoral Care* 49 (fall 1995): 329-33.

Conn, Harvie M. "Counseling in Urban Missions." *Urban Mission* 9 (1991): 3-58.

Hesselgrave, David J. "Christian Cross-Cultural Counseling: a suggested framework for theory development." *Missiology* 13 (April 1985): 203-17.

———. "Culture-Sensitive Counseling and the Christian Mission." *International Bulletin of Missionary Research* 10/3 (July 1986): 109-13.

———. "Missionary Psychology and Counseling—a timely birth." *Trinity Journal* ns 4 (spring 1983): 72-81.

Jernigan, Homer L. "Pastoral Psychotherapy in a Rapidly Changing World: Implications of Cultural Change in Singapore and Taiwan." *Therapeutic Practice in a Cross-Cultural World*: 17-34.

Karaban, Rosyln A. "Cross-Cultural Counseling: Is it Possible? Some Personal Reflections." *Pastoral Psychology* 38 (summer 1990): 219-24.

———. "Cross-Cultural Pastoral Counseling: Method or Hermeneutic? A Response." *Pastoral Psychology* 40 (March 1992): 265-69.

———. The Sharing of Cultural Variation. *Journal of Pastoral Care* 45 (spring 1991): 25-34.

Latimore, Vergel L. The Positive Contribution of Black Cultural Values to Pastoral Counseling. *Journal of Pastoral Care* 36 (June 1982): 105-17.

———. "Structures for Healing: Establishing an Outpatient Community Mental Health Center in a Minority Community." *AME Zion Quarterly Review* 95/1 (April 1983): 17-30.

Maldonado, Jorge Eduardo. "My Basic Assumptions in Pastoral Counseling of Hispanic Families." *Covenant Quarterly* 52 (May 1994): 19-28.

MacDonald, Mary N. "Some Issues in Cross-cultural Counseling." *Point* 11/2 (1982): 138-52.

Silva-Netto, Benoni. "Pastoral Counseling in a Multicultural Context." *Journal of Pastoral Care* 2 (1992): 136.

Sizemore, Barbara A. "One Blood; The Challenge of Enthnocentrism." *American Baptist Quarterly* 11 (March 1992): 50-59.

Smoke, Andrew B. "Pastoral Counseling and Black Families." *AME Zion Quarterly Review* 105 (July 1993): 26-35.

VandeCreek, Larry, and Loren Connell. "Evaluation of the Hospital Chaplain's Pastoral Care: Catholic and Protestant Differences." *Journal of Pastoral Care* 45 (fall 1991): 289-95.

Voss, Richard W. "Cross-Cultural Pastoral Counseling: Method or Hermeneutic?" *Pastoral Psychology* 40 (March 1992): 253-264.

Watson, P. J. "Apologetics and Ethnocentrism: Psychology and Religion within an Ideological Surround." *International Journal for the Psychology of Religion* 3/1 (1993): 1-20.

Weerstra, Hans M. "Member Care." *International Journal of Frantier Missions* 12 (October–December 1995): 171-223.

West, George L. "Addiction, Spirituality, and Recovery: The Role of the African American Minister." *Journal of Religious Thought* 47 (summer–fall 1990): 99-108.

Whiteman, Darrell L. "Preparation for Cross-Cultural Missions." *Missiology* 21 (January 1993): 3-75, 107-11.

Wiley, Christine Y. "A Ministry of Empowerment: A Holistic Model for Pastoral Counseling in the African American Community." *Journal of Pastoral Care* 45 (winter 1991): 355-64.

Wilson, Meretle H., and Michael R. Lyles. "Interracial Pastoral Counseling with Black Clients." *Journal of Pastoral Care* 38 (June 1984): 133-41.

Wimberly, Edward P. "Minorities." *Clinical Handbook of Pastoral Counseling*. Volume 1. New York: Paulist, 1993. 300-17.

Leading a Seminar on Multicultural, Multiracial Ministry

After understanding the challenges and prospects of multicultural, multiracial ministry, the questions that come to mind are: "How do we get this ministry started?" and "What are the tools that will guide us in this ministry?" The following section provides you with basic tools for beginning or sustaining your multicultural, multiracial ministry. Thus, you will be educating your participants with hands-on materials while equipping them to implement what they learn. This section will assist your ministry in numerous ways.

Contents

I. Obeying the Call: Conducting the Exploratory Phase

II. Getting Started: Conducting Session One

III. Understanding Culture/Comparing Cultures: Conducting Session Two

IV. Challenges: Conducting Session Three

V. Witnessing Cross-culturally: Conducting Session Four

VI. Case Studies: Conducting Session Five

VII. Worship: Conducting Session Six

I. Obeying the Call: Conducting the Exploratory Phase

The purpose of the exploratory phase is to introduce the project to the staff, leaders, and church body. This should eliminate surprises. Additionally, this phase will bridge the gap between where the church is and where the church will go. You can accomplish the phase in two steps. First, promote the project to the staff and leaders by offering testimonies and illustrations about multicultural, multiracial ministry. Solicit feedback and input from these leaders.

Next, have a church meeting the same week. For example, if you meet with the leaders on Monday night, you can meet with the church on Sunday. At the meeting, introduce the project to the church body. Present less detailed stories and illustrations about multicultural, multiracial ministries. Allow opportunities for written feedback and provide time for questions and answers. Next, pass out the Church Ownership Covenant and instruct members to check first and second choices (Appendix A). Once you determine who will serve on the focus group, send them the Focus Group Covenant (Appendix B). Also send letters to those who volunteered to pray, encourage the team, and compile information (Appendix C). Remember, the goal of the exploratory phase is to encourage the church to embrace the project. This will happen if everyone is encouraged to participate.

II. Getting Started: Conducting Session One

This first session serves as an introduction to multicultural, multiracial ministry in the local church. This will involve a discussion of the objectives of the seminar (Appendix D) and administration of a pretest to measure the group's multicultural, multiracial awareness (Appendix E).

Appendix F is a list of terms we encounter when we are involved in multicultural, multiracial ministry. Not all of these terms are used in this book; they are supplied for people who wish to further their research in this area.

Goals

The seminar leader will introduce the focus group to the study of multicultural, multiracial ministry in the local church. A pretest will be administered to measure the group's awareness of this type of ministry.

1. The seminar leader opens with prayer and then plays the seminar theme song, "Colored People" by contemporary Christian group dc Talk.

2. The seminar leader asks participants to introduce themselves and tell why they chose to be part of the focus group.

3. The pretest (Appendix E) is administered and collected.

4. The focus group is introduced to the objectives (Appendix D) and receives examples of each objective by asking stimulating questions.

Questions about Objectives (see Appendix D)

1. What is the best way to minister to different cultures from a musical perspective?

2. Can a person struggling with prejudice work with other cultures in a multicultural, multiracial church?

3. If Jesus were here among this group and spoke to us on the topic of multicultural, multiracial ministry, what do you think he would say?

4. How do you begin planning ministries and worship services for an integrated church?

5. How do you deal with the fear of witnessing cross-culturally?

Give the focus group an opportunity to ask questions about the objectives.

III. Understanding Culture/Comparing Cultures: Conducting Session Two

SESSION TWO: SEMINAR LEADER'S LESSON PLAN

Goals

To enable the focus group to understand culture and its positive and negative effects in multicultural, multiracial ministry.

Beginning Session Two

1. The seminar leader opens with prayer and then plays the project's theme song, "Colored People" by contemporary Christian group dc Talk.

2. Lead a discussion on understanding culture. Allow time for questions and answers.

3. Lead a discussion on comparing cultures. Spend a significant amount of time discussing what a cross-cultural minister should do in managing time-oriented and event-oriented situations in his or her church. Ask seminar participants to suggest recommendations for handling *time-oriented* and *event-oriented* people who attend the same church.

Ending Session Two

Consider talking about the author's experience of people calling him by his first name and by his title. Discuss how he dealt with this and what lessons can be learned from such an experience.

IV. Challenges: Conducting Session Three

This session will enable you to lead participants in discussing challenges in a multicultural, multiracial church. Many questions in this seminar require brainstorming and reflection. Additionally, because seminar participants will be challenged to explore barriers that impede and factors that cultivate relationships, they should have many questions and their participation should be at a high level. Give them an ample amount of time to make comments and ask questions.

Finally, participants will have an opportunity to review suggested ministries and tailor them according to their ministerial context. Remember, each group or congregation is different; therefore, you may adapt and modify lesson plans as you feel led.

SESSION THREE: SEMINAR LEADER'S LESSON PLAN

Goals

Seminar participants begin to develop plans for handling various challenges pastors and lay leaders confront in multicultural, multiracial churches.

Beginning Session Four

1. The seminar leader opens with prayer and then plays the project's theme song, "Colored People" by contemporary Christian group dc Talk.

2. Ask participants if God has ever turned their obstacles into opportunities. Have several people give examples of such events.

3. Discuss the Growth Challenge question: "I'm a(n) _____ (African American, white, Asian American, or Hispanic) pastor. How do I get other races to join my church?"

4. Discuss the Growth Challenge: "How do I calm the fears of particular racial groups that are not rapidly growing in our multicultural, multiracial church?"

5. Discuss the Growth Challenge question: "What lessons do we learn when the numerical growth in a multicultural, multiracial church is not rapid and how do I respond?"

6. Discuss the Worship Challenge question: "How do multicultural, multiracial churches meet people's needs in worship without making such a challenge the primary goal of worship?"

7. Discuss the Worship Challenge question: "Is it possible to find one music minister who can minister effectively to different races? What do multicultural, multiracial churches do if such individuals cannot be found?"

8. Discuss the Staying Challenged question: "How do we prevent particular racial groups from leaving multicultural, multiracial churches?"

Ending Session Three

Give seminar participants an opportunity to discuss other challenges pastors and lay leaders encounter in multicultural, multiracial churches.

V. Witnessing Cross-culturally: Conducting Session Four

Encourage participants to give a testimony involving a time in which they shared their faith with someone of a different race or culture. Lead them in discussing the vitality of lay ministry positions for establishing and nurturing a multicultural, multiracial church.

SESSION FOUR: SEMINAR LEADER'S LESSON PLAN

Goals

The seminar participants understand various methods of witnessing cross-culturally. Additionally, they will prepare themselves for assessing their own ministry and lay leadership needs.

Beginning Session Four

1. The seminar leader opens with prayer and then plays the project's theme song, "Colored People" by contemporary Christian group dc Talk.

2. Use the following Scripture passages to discuss principles of cross-cultural witnessing found in the Bible:
   • Acts 17:22-34
   • John 4:1-30

3. Guide the participants in reviewing lay ministry job descriptions currently available in their church and those that may be needed.

4. Develop an assessment form (like that in Appendix G) and review it. Discuss how the sheet might be implemented in their ministry context.

Ending Session Four

Give participants an opportunity to discuss challenges they face when hiring staff. Also, talk about the pros and cons of using volunteer ministry workers.

VI. Case Studies: Conducting Session Five

For session five of your multicultural, multiracial seminar, lead participants into exploring various case studies you prepare beforehand that might be at issue in your particular church as it attempts to grow multiculturally. The case studies should consider real difficulties involving multicultural, multiracial situations. Guide small groups of participants to develop plans of their own for handling each case study situation. (An alternate plan is to have each small group consider a different case study.) After small groups have ample opportunity to develop plans for each case study, allow time for discussion of plans.

Each case study should have five parts. First, summarize the situation, the people involved, and the difficulty encountered. Second, diagnose the real issue. Third, describe the interventions attempted, their results, and a critique of those attempts. Fourth, seek a biblical understanding of the theological issues involved. Finally, present a plan for pastoral and lay care. (Sample case studies and participant small group responses can be found in Appendix H).

VII. Worship: Conducting Session Six

In this last seminar, you will guide participants to understand how to plan worship services for their growing multiracial, multicultural congregation.

SESSION SIX: SEMINAR LEADER'S LESSON PLAN

Goals

To enable the participants to plan worship services for multicultural, multiracial churches. Additionally, they will be exposed to different worship styles among traditional homogeneous congregations and emerging integrated congregations.

Two Weeks Prior to Session Six

1. The first week, have participants visit one traditional non-White church. The second week, have participants visit a traditional White church. The purpose of these visits is to compare the distinct congregations.

2. Instruct participants to enter the churches in no more than twos or threes. Be sure that groups of participants sit in separate areas within the worship center.

3. A few hours prior to the beginning of session six, view on videotape the worship service of a local multicultural, multiracial church, if possible. You may contact multicultural, multiracial churches in your local area to request a copy of any available videotaped service. Some local services may be available over local television stations.

Beginning Session Six

1. The seminar leader opens with prayer and then plays the project's theme song, "Colored People" by contemporary Christian group dc Talk.

2. Lead a general discussion on the distinct worship styles viewed in the previous two weeks' visits to other worship services.

3. Guide the participants in evaluating and analyzing the diverse congregations (Appendix I).

Ending Session Six

Give participants an opportunity to plan a worship service for a multicultural, multiracial church within their local church setting.

Appendixes

Appendix A

CHURCH OWNERSHIP COVENANT

Name: _____

Date: _____

I am between the ages (optional):

❑ 14-21   ❑ 22-35   ❑ 36-45   ❑ 46-55   ❑ Over 55

I will take ownership of the seminar by:

1. ❑ Praying for the seminar daily
    ❑ Praying for the seminar once a week
    ❑ Praying for the seminar once a month
    ❑ Other. Please indicate how you will pray:

    _____

    _____

    _____

    _____

    _____

2. ❑ Compiling information

3. ❑ Attending the focus group meetings for thirteen weeks

4. ❑ Encouraging the focus group weekly by word and deed

Appendix B

FOCUS GROUP COVENANT

As a member of the focus group, I commit myself to:

1. Congregate at all sessions unless prevented by unforeseen circumstances. In the event I'm unable to attend, I agree to make up the session with the seminar leader.

2. Participate in each session by offering fresh insights and ideas to the concept of multicultural, multiracial ministry.

3. Evaluate the material and offer suggestions for the enhancement of the multicultural, multiracial church.

4. Dedicate myself to prayer, asking God for his blessings on the focus group and his church as we seek his will for the enhancement of diversity in this local church and the Body of Christ.

Focus Group Member's Signature: _____

Date: _____

Appendix C

LETTERS TO SEMINAR PARTICIPANTS

Date
Focus Group Member's Name
Street Address
City, State, and Zip

Dear Member,

I am excited about the new opportunity you and I have to strengthen our church through enhancing our multicultural, multiracial ministry. A great deal of time and effort has already gone into the preparation of this ministry. I am looking forward to learning with you as we embark on one of the most exciting ministries of the twenty-first century!

As is the case with any learning experience, your ***attendance***, ***participation***, and ***feedback*** in these training sessions are vital. I am enclosing a seminar schedule and a focus group covenant for you to examine. If you have questions about either one, please contact me. If not, please sign the covenant and send it back to me in the enclosed envelope. Also, the times for the sessions can easily be adjusted depending on the needs of focus group members. Please let me know ***as soon as possible*** if there is a conflict with the presented schedule.

I realize that there will be instances when you will possibly have to miss a session. In that case, arrangements will be made for you to make up the session.

Thank you for prayerfully considering being part of the focus group. I believe this seminar is going to bless [YOUR CHURCH] beyond measure. We are going to have an exciting time!

Thanks for your service,
Your Pastor

Appendix C1

Date
Dear Member:

Thank you so much for committing to encourage the group for our seminar on pastoral and lay care in a multicultural, multiracial church ministry. The objective is to call or personally contact each member once a week and encourage them as they participate in the training sessions.

Your support will be very important to the group and to [YOUR CHURCH] as we begin this seminar.

God Bless,
Your Pastor

Appendix C2

Date
Dear Member:

Thank you for committing to pray for our seminar on pastoral and lay care in a multicultural, multiracial church ministry. Your prayer support is very important to the attending group and to [YOUR CHURCH] as we begin this seminar.

God Bless,
Your Pastor

Appendix C3

Date
Dear Member:

Thank you so much for committing to assist in compiling information for our seminar on pastoral and lay care in a multicultural, multiracial church ministry.

At this point, it is difficult to measure the amount of compilation involved in the seminar. Your participation in this area, if necessary, will most likely be toward the end of the seminar. However, thank you for praying as you've indicated on your covenant card.

I greatly appreciate you!

God Bless,
Your Pastor

Appendix D

SEMINAR OBJECTIVES

This seminar is about analyzing methods of pastoral and lay care in a multicultural, multiracial church. Biblical and practical responses to multicultural, multiracial ministry will be evaluated.

Objectives

Upon completion of this seminar, the participants and church members should:

A. Understand the nature and concept of multicultural, multiracial ministry in the local church.
B. Recognize the need for multicultural, multiracial churches.
C. Understand the challenges of ministering in a multicultural, multiracial congregation.
D. Identify barriers that impede relational and numerical growth in a multicultural, multiracial congregation.
E. Formulate a personal philosophy for multicultural, multiracial ministry, based on biblical instruction and examples.
F. Plan and implement worship services and ministries that meet needs in a culturally diverse church.
G. Explore various methods of evangelizing cross-culturally.
H. Organize ministries that foster and nurture cross-cultural, cross-racial relationships.
I. Serve in a multicultural, multiracial church.
J. Provide personal care in a multicultural, multiracial church.
K. Develop a continuing personal study of multicultural, multiracial church ministries.

Appendix E

SESSION ONE PRETEST

Answer true or false.

T / F 1. In a multicultural, multiracial church, Christianity takes precedence over cultural distinctions.

T / F 2. People attending multicultural, multiracial churches do not struggle with racism.

T / F 3. Communication is important when establishing cross-cultural relationships.

T / F 4. Jesus ministered cross-culturally.

T / F 5. A multicultural, multiracial church is built on a firm foundation of love.

T / F 6. It is solely the pastor's job to minister in a multicultural, multiracial church.

T / F 7. God expects people of all cultures to be reconciled to each other.

In your own words, explain the following phrases:

8. multicultural, multiracial church—

9. homogeneous church—

Listing

10. List three Scriptures that support the idea of having love for all people.

11. List two passages that show the kingdom's culture having supremacy over our individual cultures.

12. List one example in the New Testament of someone ministering cross-culturally.

Pretest: Answer Key

Answer true or false.

T 1. In a multicultural, multiracial church, Christianity takes precedence over cultural distinctions.

F 2. People attending multicultural, multiracial churches do not struggle with racism.

T 3. Communication is important when establishing cross-cultural relationships.

T 4. Jesus ministered cross-culturally.

T 5. A multicultural, multiracial church is built on a firm foundation of love.

F 6. It is solely the pastor's job to minister in a multicultural, multiracial church.

T 7. God expects people of all races to be reconciled to each other.

In your own words, explain the following phrase:

8. multicultural, multiracial church—*a church that includes a noticeable presence of at least two culturally diverse groups that serve the Lord together in ministry and honor the Lord together in worship.*

9. homogeneous church—*a church comprised of one race or culture that serves the Lord together in ministry and honors the Lord together in worship.*

Listing

10. List three Scriptures that support the idea of having love for all people.
Answers will vary

11. List two passages that show the kingdom's culture superseding our individual cultures.
Answers will vary

12. List one example in the New Testament of someone ministering cross-culturally.
Answers will vary

Appendix F

TERMINOLOGY

Culturally Diverse Groups

Ethnic: originally meant a number of people living together; later meant a tribe, a people, a nation, or a group

Ethnicity: the part of cultural development that occurs prior to the onset of a child's abstract intellectual powers as a result of his direct, personal contacts with the people around him and with his immediate environment

Ethnic group: any group demarcated by one or more categories of race, religion, or national origin

Minority: a group of people who, because of their physical or cultural characteristics, are singled out from others in the society in which they live for differential and unequal treatment and who therefore regard themselves as objects of collective discrimination

Sociological Perspective

Acculturation: the process by which people learn to adapt to the general culture while still maintaining their own particular subcultures

Assimilation: the process by which adults are inducted into a new culture through conversion, thereby leaving behind the first culture into which they had been enculturated

Biculturalization: the blending of two cultures, keeping some learned characteristics of each and in time giving birth to a new cultural expression

Enculturation: a natural process of formal and informal intentional and unintentional means by which children are inducted into a community and acquire its culture

Ideological Perspective

Cultural relativism: emphasizes the values within other cultures without reference or comparison to those of our own

Deconstructionism: holds that the best way to create equality is simply to dismantle the institutions of the previous social majority

Ethnocentrism: the tendency to view the norms and values of one's own culture as absolute and to use them as a standard against which to judge and measure all other cultures

Halfway pluralism: preserves distinctives related to family and family values but allows interaction within the broader community of commerce and education

Insular pluralism: cultural groups retreat from society at large to preserve their social unit

Intercultural communication: attempts a reconciliation between ethnocentrism and pluralism. It denotes the understanding that takes place whenever the sender is a member of one culture and the receiver is a member of another. The term is also known as cross-cultural communication, interethnic communication, or trans-racial communication.

Pluralism: synonymous with cultural relativism; sees all cultures as equally valid in claims concerning religion, values, and ultimate meaning

Postmodernism: the precommitment to relativism or pluralism in relation to questions of truth

Structural assimilation: deals with differences by diminishing or even eliminating them. Emphasis is on an open society that cuts across all divisions of religion, culture, or race

Social Attitudes

Discrimination: differential behavior directed toward a group. Acts of discrimination occur when people are treated in an inequitable manner because they belong to a certain group.

Prejudice: a set of rigid and unfavorable attitudes toward a particular group or groups

Prejudiced discriminator: does not believe in values of freedom and equality and consistently discriminates against other groups in both word and deed

Prejudiced nondiscriminator: feels hostile to other groups but recognizes that law and social pressures are opposed to overt discrimination. Reluctantly, this person does not translate prejudice into action.

Racism: constitutes attitudes, beliefs, and policies practiced when a group has the power to enforce laws, institutions, and norms based on its beliefs, which oppress and dehumanize another group

Unprejudiced discriminator: not personally prejudiced, but may sometimes, reluctantly, discriminate against other groups because it seems socially or financially convenient to do so

Unprejudiced nondiscriminator: upholds American ideals of freedom and equality in both belief and practice. This person is not prejudiced against other groups and, on principle, does not discriminate against them.

Appendix G

SAMPLE GIFTS, TALENTS, AND SKILLS ASSESSMENT FORM

Name: _____

Address: _____

Telephone: _____

Best time to call: _____

I would be willing to participate in the following ministries:

1. A.M.E.N. (men's)
2. Awana (children's)
3. Children's Choir
4. Children's Church
5. Church Choir
6. Church Greeter
7. Church Usher
8. Decision Counseling
9. Discipleship
10. ESL (English Tutor)
11. Evangelism
12. IV Ministry
   (Internal Visitation)
13. Missions
14. Prayer
15. Singles
16. Sunday School Worker
17. Tape Ministry
18. Union Gospel
   (Ministry to Homeless)
19. Visitation Ministry
20. Women's Ministry
21. Youth Ministry
22. Youth Choir
23. I Need Help With Assessing
   My Gifts
24. Other
   _____

List any special skills, training, or knowledge that you have:

_____

_____

_____

Appendix H

SAMPLE CASE STUDIES

Sample Case Study 1: Cindy

Cindy has been an active member of the church for the past 6 years. She is now 13 and in the 8th grade. The majority of children at the church are African American, and Cindy has often been the only white child there. This has not been an issue in the past in establishing friendships.

Cindy is active in youth choir, attends Sunday school regularly, and participates in other activities when she is able. She began attending the Wednesday night program last year but has not been interested in participating this year. She says she has no one to "hang out with," and she feels left out—having to sit by herself, feeling ignored by the other youth, and so forth.

Cindy went to camp with the youth group last summer. She had a good experience and felt she got to know some of the other girls better. However, the relationships have not continued or grown back at home. Cindy found that her values differ quite a bit from some of the other girls, and this may contribute to the problem. However, it does not seem to affect her friendships at school.

We have tried to arrange opportunities for Cindy and other girls from the church to spend time together, but this has not strengthened relationships between them.

Cindy has considered opportunities to attend other churches where she has friends and will feel more comfortable in activities. She does not seem to have negative feelings about her experience at our church, although she did last year. She says she knows it could be much worse and that the kids are not mean to her. She desires to feel like a real part of the youth group, but she sees no way to make that happen.

Other white teen girls have come through the youth group, but none have felt accepted and they have not continued attending. It should be noted that there are several African American youth in our membership who also do not participate in youth activities.

SAMPLE SMALL GROUP'S CASE STUDY REPORT

Brief Description of the Problem

Cindy attends a multicultural, multiracial church in which the youth group is mostly African American. In fact, she is the only active white teen. She feels alienated and left out of the group. She cannot find a way to fit in. Often the youth are given the responsibility of contacting other youth regarding activities, but Cindy is not informed about these opportunities. Although she continues to participate in the youth activities, she is considering visiting other churches where she already has friends. Her parents have made attempts to assist Cindy in establishing relationships, but these have not been effective. It should be noted that there are other teens from active families in the church who do not participate in youth activities.

Presenting the Problem

1. Cindy feels excluded from group.
2. She wants to be a part of the youth, but her attempts to do so have been unsuccessful.
3. Cindy feels her personal values are at odds with those in the youth group.
4. Cindy is shy.
5. One must consider that teens typically tend to form exclusive groups.
6. Cindy is thinking of attending other churches.

Descriptions of Interventions Attempted

1. Cindy has remained active in the church and youth activities in an attempt to make friends.
2. Her parents have provided opportunities for her to be with other girls in the youth group.
3. The parents have consulted with the youth pastor several times.

Biblical and Theological Issues

1. If the youth are more concerned with themselves than with others, they should not (Rom 12:13).
2. Everyone should be included in the fellowship (Luke 14:12-14).
3. Our oneness in Christ supersedes cultural distinctions (Gal 3:28).

4. Cindy needs to be content and trust that the situation will improve (Heb 13:5).

5. Kindness is necessary (Eph 4:32).

Plan for Pastoral and Lay Care

1. Pray for God's will and guidance in this situation.

2. Encourage Cindy to stay involved.

3. Tell Cindy that she does not need to change values to make friends.

4. The youth minister should meet with Cindy and her parents to offer encouragement and get feedback.

5. Do not over-exaggerate the issue; cliques are a normal, though painful, part of adolescent life.

6. Educate the youth group on inclusiveness, reaching across barriers, and sensitivity.

7. Intentionally plan activities with the youth to provide inclusiveness and fellowship.

8. Plan activities with other youth groups with white members.

Sample Case Study 2: Interracial Teen Couple

Two teenagers are in what they consider a serious relationship. They have begun to think about going to college together. They are 16 and 17 years old. The teenage boy and girl truly love one another. The boy's parents have no problem with their son's relationship. Each of them (the boy, his parents, and the girl) attends the same church. The girl's parents do not attend church at all. They want their daughter to stop seeing her boyfriend. In fact, they want her to stop attending the church and seeing her boyfriend because he is white and she is African American.

The youth minister has counseled both teenagers. However, he is seeking direction on how to counsel these two people further. The girl has been growing spiritually, but now she is told to stop coming to church.

SAMPLE SMALL GROUP'S CASE STUDY REPORT

Brief Description of the Problem

A teen boy and girl (ages 16 and 17) are in a serious interracial relationship. They attend the same church. The girl's parents do not attend church. They are against the relationship. They want their daughter to stop seeing the young man and stop attending the church.

The youth minister has counseled the teens. He has seen spiritual growth in the young lady and is concerned about her leaving the church.

Presenting the Problem

1. Two teens are involved in a serious interracial relationship.
2. Both teens and the boy's parents attend the same church.
3. The girl's parents do not attend church.
4. The girl's parents are against the interracial relationship and want it to be terminated.
5. The girl's parents want their daughter to stop attending the church and avoid contact with the boy.
6. The girl is growing spiritually at the church. The youth minister wants to know how he should handle the situation. He is concerned because he led the girl to Christ. Also, this is the only church she has ever attended.

Description of Attempted Intervention

The youth minister has counseled the girl and the boy.

Biblical and Theological Issues

1. The girl is disobeying her parents' wishes, and the parents are provoking the girl (Eph 6:1-4).
2. The girl would be disobeying Scripture by not attending church (Heb 10:25).
3. The girl's parents do not understand that God does not judge us according to our cultural or racial profile (Gal 3:28).
4. The girl's parents are not saved.
5. The church cannot tell the girl to disobey her parents.

Plan for Pastoral and Lay Care

1. Encourage the youth minister to pray for the girl and her parents.
2. Counsel the teens to be patient regarding their relationship and feelings.
3. Have the pastor meet with the teens and the boy's parents.
4. Invite the unchurched parents to church.
5. Assure that the girl's spiritual growth is given priority.
6. Find another church for the girl to attend. Help her during the transition.

Appendix I

WORSHIP SERVICE EVALUATION FORM

A. How is your church similar to the other church(es) you visited?

B. How is your church different from the other church(es) you visited?

C. What are some distinguishing features of the church(es) you visited?

D. What did you like and/or dislike about the church(es) you visited?

E. If you could add something to your church from the church(es) you visited, what would it be?